62 SENIOR MOMENTS

True, inspirational stories about seniors
62 and older whose lives were changed for
the better because of a reverse mortgage

Sam Collins

62 Senior Moments

ISBN-13 978-0-9798791-0-4

ISBN-10 0-9798791-0-8

Printed in the United States of America

Equal Housing
Lender

Disclaimer

The information contained in this book is for informational purposes only and the Publisher makes no representation or guarantee that you will find this information to be satisfactory, effective, complete, or be of benefit for your own particular circumstances. The Publisher makes no recommendation regarding reverse mortgage transactions, does not have the intention to give financial, legal, or any other type of professional advice, and this information is not intended to replace financial, legal or any other type of professional advice. You are advised to consult with a professional for any actual reserve mortgage transaction in which you are involved.

All chapters in this book are stories related by third parties. The Publisher cannot and does not represent or warrant the veracity, qualifications, skills, credentials, and experience of any content provider, nor does it authenticate, guarantee the appropriateness, accuracy, and reliability or endorse the information provided

Foreword

Experiencing the joy of giving is much better than receiving. Such was the case I envisioned when the idea of writing this book and sharing with other seniors the realities of what senior homeowners across the United States experienced after having completed a reverse mortgage or Home Equity Conversion Mortgage (HECM).

Homeownership in America is one of our most cherished dreams and treasured assets. Many of you have worked hard to earn the right to be called "homeowners," and as a nation, we should be eternally grateful for the sacrifices you have made to provide us with the freedoms and opportunities we all enjoy in our lives.

For most of us, our home is the largest investment we will make in our lifetime. Decisions regarding our home and family are not to be taken lightly. Life has taught us that education and experience are the best teachers. Reading these stories of what others have experienced will provide you with the knowledge to fully understand the real truth about reverse mortgages.

62 Senior Moments is a collection of real-life stories about mature senior homeowners just like you and me. These heartwarming stories may impact your life in more ways than you thought imaginable. You will discover that reverse mortgages can be used for many different reasons.

Since our needs, wants, desires, and situations are individually different, we often feel no one else is experiencing the same thing. For this reason, I am sure you will be able to relate with many others in this book.

Acknowledgments

In putting together *62 Senior Moments*, I am most indebted to my wife, Peggy, for having the patience to persevere with me and understand the journey to get from 0 to 62 stories. A heartfelt thanks goes out to my four children and family who have faith in my ideas and give me the inspiration to achieve higher expectations.

My indefatigable editor, Julie Taylor, was invaluable to me, continually reminding me of the value of our quest and the importance of sharing real-life stories that outline the benefits a reverse mortgage offers to senior homeowners. Julie's steady perseverance kept this book on schedule and true to our mission, culminating over a year of hard work.

A special thanks to Becki Lathem, my assistant, who was diligent in keeping accurate, timely records. Becki's attention to detail and positive attitude helped make this project a success.

Thanks also to our storytellers, our reverse mortgage professionals, who through their good works, deeds, professionalism, and dedication to improving the lives of seniors make this book and its stories come to life. Compassion, understanding, and doing the right thing for our senior homeowners is an inspiration to all who provide services to seniors clients.

Thanks to all the originators who talked to me about their experiences and involvement in sharing stories of why they love working with seniors. Thanks to the entire body of reverse mortgage professionals throughout the U.S. who understand the importance respect we owe our senior clients, and those who attest to maintaining the highest of ethical and moral standards.

Thanks to the Department of Housing and Urban Development (HUD) and the Federal Housing Administration (FHA) for understanding the needs of our U.S. senior homeowner taxpayers and working tirelessly to implement the Housing and Economic Recovery Act and providing guidelines for its clarification.

Thanks to all of our legislators who worked to enact the Housing and Economic Recovery Act so that it will provide invaluable assistance to more of our senior homeowners to utilize a reverse mortgage.

Putting together 62 stories was not an easy task and took a lot of time. In our case, these stories were over a year in the making. During this period of time, a multitude of changes occurred within our economy, with new legislation, within our government, culminating with the election of our new President. All these changes have profound effects on our maturing population. I hope this book will be a shining light to show there are options for our senior homeowners, and it is my hope for them to be happy, secure, and worry free.

We, as a nation, should be eternally grateful for the good deeds of our mature population and sacrifices they have made to make our lives and freedoms what they are today.

Contents

Chapter

1

Sam Collins
Delaware Financial Capital Corp.

THE LOVE BETWEEN MOTHER
AND DAUGHTER ENDURES

(Story told by Sam Collins, Reverse Mortgage Professional)

I am often asked if the children of parents who do a reverse mortgage agree with their parent's decision. I have found that when children understand the benefits of this powerful program, they are very supportive of their parents. Ultimately, children of parents who qualify for a reverse mortgage want what is best for their Mother and Father. They want their parents to be worry free and enjoy their golden years.

Joyce (daughter) and Christine (mother), are two clients whose story I want to share with you and is a wonderful example of how a reverse mortgage can benefit both mother and daughter.

Almost four years ago, while driving her Mother, Christine, from her home in Delaware back to Joyce's home in Florida, Joyce began to notice that her Mother was acting out of character. Joyce used her good judgment, turned her car around and headed back to Delaware. She immediately took her mother to the hospital, where she was admitted. Joyce later discovered her Mother was experiencing mini strokes, but unfortunately the next day, her mom, Christine, experienced a stroke. The stroke left Christine partially paralyzed on her right side and her speech was also impaired.

Joyce told me that she and her mother both felt lucky. Joyce said if she had not returned to Delaware, the outcome could have been a lot worse for her Mother. Also, returning to Delaware enabled her Mother to be near her friends and stay in the home where she felt most comfortable and where she had lived for the past 50 years.

Joyce was now left with a major decision. She was the only child and realized her mother needed her to stay in Delaware and provide the best quality life and care possible. After living in Florida for 38 years, Joyce decided the decision was clear; she would return to Delaware and help care for her mother. Joyce was not exactly sure how her and her Mother would make ends meet financially but, were determined to find a way. This was after- all, her mother and nothing was going to stop her from providing the best possible care for her.

Joyce had heard about reverse mortgages from television and other advertisements but, did not quite understand exactly how they worked or how the reverse mortgage might work for her situation so, she decided to so some research. Based on her initial research, Joyce thought a reverse mortgage might be a good alternative to relieve their financial stress and discussed the possibility with her mother. Her mom agreed it made sense to pursue the option of doing a reverse mortgage, but wanted more facts.

I first spoke with Joyce when she called our office and requested more information about reverse mortgages. I immediately went to see her and her mother the next day and hand delivered an informational video, which explained the in and outs of a reverse mortgage.

Our first meeting was wonderful. If you are having a bad day, you might consider giving Joyce and Christine a visit. They have got to be two of the most positive and upbeat people I have ever met. They were laughing from the time I arrived until the time I left. Considering the financial strains they were under, I was even more impressed with their positive outlook on life.

When income is constrained, it doesn't take long for time to eat away at every possible asset. Soon when debt exceeds income, each month becomes more and more difficult. Joyce and Christine were managing, but barely. They had little money left over at the end of each month and absolutely no money available to make repairs or home improvements.

Sometimes things have a way of working out. During my visit I found out Joyce (daughter) was 62, which made it possible for her, as well as her Mother, to also qualify for a reverse mortgage. Mrs. Stephenson (Mother) decided she wanted to add her daughter to the deed which in essence made her an equal owner of the home and since she was 62, she was eligible to do a reverse mortgage, along with her Mother. Since both Mother and daughter were eligible to do a reverse mortgage, this turned out to be a very beneficial solution for Joyce and her Mother. Joyce was now able to stay in Delaware, take care of her Mother, and stay in the home they both owned for as long as either of them wanted to live and stay.

When we reviewed the different reverse mortgage options, we realized Joyce and Christine were again very fortunate. There was a considerable amount of equity in their home. Mother and daughter were going to be able to payoff a small home equity loan (2nd mortgage), payoff all their credit card debt and still have a considerable amount of money left over. Our Mother and daughter team had plans to replace their kitchen, dining, room and family room flooring and paint all three rooms.

The benefits continue to get even better for our Mom and daughter team. Our analysis showed when they paid off their home equity loan and credit card debt that it made a huge impact on their monthly and annual increase in cash. The increase in spendable cash flow represented a large portion of their current income. Once the reverse mortgage was completed they could afford to do things they wanted without the worry of just scrimping by from month to month.

Joyce said she highly recommended more seniors should consider the benefits they can get by doing a reverse mortgage. She said she has recommended a reverse mortgage to several of her friends. "Most seniors I know are slow to go ahead, but when they truly understand, they may change their mind." Joyce said. "You need to enjoy everyday of your life, don't wait, so why not use your home to help you, and the best part is you get to stay in the home you love."

The most impressive part of having done this reverse mortgage was to see the love and trust that was evident in this great relationship between a Mother and her daughter. Joyce is to be admired for walking away from 38 years of her life in Florida and devoting herself to her Mother's care.

> "Daughters understand as they grow older,
> they become good friends." *Catherine Pulsifer*

About Sam Collins

1-877-266-9500
www.reversemortagesforyou.com
www.seniorsrighttoknow.com

Sam Collins is the President of Delaware Financial Capital Corp, a licensed mortgage banker, specializing in the reverse mortgage business and is committed to improving the lives of seniors. Sam has owned his own businesses for over 38 years and is considered a reverse mortgage industry leader and advocates to always do the right thing for his senior clients. Sam has four children and makes his home in Delaware. Contact Sam scollins@delawarefinancial.com or call 800-242-5085 for his Free report and DVD, "Ins and Outs of a Reverse Mortgage."

Chapter

2

Bradford Financial, Inc. and
Law Offices of Chris Albanese, LLC

THE ANSWER TO OUR PRAYER

(Story told by the Senior Client)

Are there enough boxes to fill thirty-nine years of memories? Our friends seemed to think so. I couldn't tell you how many times we heard them tell us to stop wasting our time and start packing. Our house, our home was set for auction the following Saturday. Unless something happened, virtually instantaneously; we were going to be thrown out. Where would we go? The only upside of this terrible situation was that we wouldn't have to worry about how to pay the mortgage anymore.

By the time you added up all of the bills, at the end of the month, there was not enough money to pay for the prescription medication that the insurance company did not cover. My husband and I could either pay our mortgage payment or pay for medication and food. Forced to choose between paying for medication and making the mortgage payment was like being caught between a rock and a hard place. There was no money for the basics, let alone extras. To make matters worse, our house was in terrible need of repair, however, hiring a painter or contractor was not exactly in the budget. Although it was spring, one of our favorite seasons, we were scared, frustrated, angry and very sad.

It was a sunny morning and we could see the deer on our front lawn and in the field across the road nibbling on grass as we sat around the kitchen table. Staring into our half empty coffee cups with heavy hearts, we started to reminisce about how much had changed in our neighborhood. We just couldn't believe that in a little over one week from now our home would be purchased by a stranger at an auction. We tried everything we could think of to save our home. We talked to our creditors, went without necessities and even ordered a DVD from a commercial we saw on television about reverse mortgages. Unfortunately, nothing worked. Our creditors didn't care – they just wanted their money. We never got the DVD or any other information about a reverse mortgage from that company. The guy who was supposed to send it to us went on vacation or something. It was clear he really didn't care about our situation.

Sandy, a close family friend, drove by our house and saw the auction sign on our front lawn. She immediately encouraged us to contact Ann Marie Savona and Glenn Johnson at Bradford Financial.

She assured us that anything was possible and if there was a chance to save our home, Ann Marie and Glenn were the ones to help do it. As a last resort, on a hope and a prayer, we took Sandy's advice and made the call.

During the initial telephone conversation, Glenn expressed how he could hear the desperation in our voices. He said he could almost feel the anxiety through the phone line. It seemed as though we were on the same page because we were indeed desperate and anxious. Glenn continued to assure us that there was still hope for saving our home and a reverse mortgage would be the vehicle he and his partner would use. He answered all of our initial questions, took time to explain what a reverse mortgage was and how it worked. We thought it sounded too good to be true but certainly wanted to pursue it as it might just be the answer to our prayers. Glenn gave us specific instructions and we gathered the information needed for the paperwork. We set an appointment to meet later that same day.

During our first meeting, we explained how we got into such an uncomfortable financial situation and once again expressed concern if the solution being discussed would even work. We tried to stay hopeful but we were doubtful, as we had already resigned ourselves to the harsh reality that our house was gone forever. After listening to our story and gaining a better understanding of our financial situation, Glenn and Ann Marie assured us there was an opportunity to save our home from foreclosure. Using a reverse mortgage, the goal was for us to pay off the existing mortgage, eliminating all future mortgage payments and hold back $10,000 for necessary repairs in order for the house to pass inspection. It was simply amazing that we would also have a few thousand dollars left to use for emergencies so we never had to find ourselves in a similar situation.

Outside of the needed repairs and tight budget, our particular loan scenario was a bit out of the norm. Herbert and I are lucky that Ann Marie and Glenn have backgrounds as financial planners. They pride themselves in conducting a thorough discovery process in evaluating how a reverse mortgage ties in with every other financial product their clients may have. There was a significant age difference between Herbert and myself and I was not yet 62. Normally, the folks at Bradford Financial would not recommend a reverse mortgage with such an age difference, however, in this case our house was set for auction; it was as good as gone. The required HUD counseling was scheduled the next day.

With a lot of work to do in a very short period of time, Ann Marie and Glenn focused their attention on coordinating meetings with various home improvement professionals. They personally contacted an appraiser, contractor and termite inspector so each vendor could work together to determine what outstanding work was necessary to bring the house up to code. The list of repairs included replacing windows and painting the entire house. Every penny counted! The contractors were made aware they had to be very flexible and willing to reduce their prices. One contractor in particular Howard Smith, with Smith General Contracting (860-961-7604) was extremely helpful in offering reduced rates to help us as much as he could. Time and money were luxuries we just didn't have. Ann Marie and Glenn rolled up their sleeves and got dirty. They were able to save us even more money by personally taking the necessary water samples and driving them to the lab to get the test results.

We were scheduled to close our reverse mortgage, a loan that would save our home from foreclosure. It was now time for Real Estate Attorney, Chris Albanese to do his part. Ann Marie and Glenn explained to us that for the past five years they worked closely with self-employed Real Estate Attorney, Chris Albanese. Chris oversaw all Bradford Financial loan closings. We were definitely in very good hands as Attorney Albanese is experienced in dealing with closings entangled in foreclosure proceedings.

Four days after their very first meeting, the professionals at Bradford Financial and Attorney Chris Albanese closed our loan and saved our house from foreclosure. Attorney Albanese described the loan closing best when he said "There was not a dry-eye in my office. This was such an emotional experience for every one. The Willey's had virtually lost their home and now they were able to fix up their house and are still living there today. It's the only time in my life I've been told I'm the answer to somebody's prayers. Most people don't say that to an attorney!"

About Us

Bradford Financial, Inc. and
Law Offices of Chris Albanese, LLC
185 Boston Post Road
Waterford, CT 06385
www.bradford-financial.com
1-800-309-0472

The Law Office of Chris Albanese LLC
1600 Route 12, Second Floor
Gales Ferry, CT 06335
www.albanese-law.com
860-464-1200

The professionals Bradford Financial, Inc. offers comprehensive financial strategies and recognizes the reverse mortgage as a financial tool and know how it fits in with every other financial product our clients have. Partners Ann Marie Savona and Glenn B. Johnson are Certified Senior Advisors and Reverse Mortgage Specialists.

The Law Office of Chris Albanese specializes in real estate law. We are a cost competitive, client friendly closing team. We do all closings from the simple to complex, including those entangled in foreclosure proceedings. Residential transactions consist of about 80% of the business. Additional practice areas are commercial real estate, limited liability company formation for real estate investors & others, title searching, and wills & trusts.

Chapter
3

Mike Mertel
Senior Solutions

ONE LAST WISH

(Story told by the Senior Client)

Judy had just arrived home from a walk and I knew she would be livid when I told her we needed to leave. I had signed us up for a financial seminar, which I forgot to tell her about. The seminar was focused on ways seniors could reduce their health care costs, grow their assets, and provide answers to many different financial questions. The flyer advertising the seminar listed reverse mortgages; something I was particularly interested in. Besides, it was being held at a nice restaurant and we could use a night out on someone else's dime. I told Judy about the seminar and she laughed at me, saying "We don't have any money. Why are we going to a financial seminar?" I simply smiled and told her to get in the car. I am so thankful she listened to me.

My main motive for attending the seminar was shear desperation. Recently, we had found ourselves in an extremely unfavorable financial predicament. For years I owned a successful business, which allowed us to build a beautiful home in an extremely desirable neighborhood just outside of Kansas City – Lee's Summit. I provided a good life for my family until a few months ago; I was diagnosed with cancer. I had quickly become extremely ill, and was now unable to work. As a small business owner, if you are not working, the business is not making any money. This was not something we were prepared for.

All of our household expenses continued to pile up, including our mortgage payment. We had burned through our savings, investments, and to put it mildly, we were in desperate straits. I was not having success in beating my illness, so I redirected my focus toward my family. Primarily, I was concerned about how Judy would survive financially after I passed away; as I had always been the primary breadwinner of our family. I did not want her lifestyle to change because of my illness.

There was absolutely no way Judy would be able to afford the monthly mortgage payment of $1,500, along with property taxes, utilities, and regular living expenses on her own. I was determined to make certain my loving wife could remain in the home, full of our memories. Judy deserved to grieve in her home, not a rented apartment or someone else's house. We needed help; yet time was a luxury we did not have.

By the time we arrived at the seminar, Judy was in a sassy mood to say the least. She was not happy and made it clear to everyone that she was an unwilling participant. As the seminar progressed, and we started to learn about reverse mortgages, Judy's demeanor changed. Mike Mertel from Senior Solutions was very impressive and knowledgeable. I was most impressed by his philosophy on reverse mortgages: "I (Mike Mertel) want people to understand that reverse mortgages are not just for people in financial trouble or for those who need money. They are for people who want to pass on money, to take care of their families. A reverse mortgage is for people who want to do the things they always dreamed of doing but, either did not have the time or resources." I felt as though Mike was speaking directly to me and said a silent prayer of thanks for the divine intervention I was experiencing.

By the end of the seminar, I could not wait to schedule an appointment with Mike to discuss how a reverse mortgage might work for us. A reverse mortgage sounded like the solution needed to dig Judy and myself out of debt and allow her to stay in our home. We were scheduled to meet with Mike three days later.

During our ride home, Judy expressed some concerns she had regarding what we heard. Her skepticism was that a reverse mortgage seemed too good to be true. She feared this could be a situation in which we would be disappointed and more heartache was the last thing either of us needed. We were in such a desperate place both financially and emotionally that it became hard to believe we could actually get out of it. When your spouse is dying, it is an extremely emotional situation, you stop trusting yourself with important decisions because you are distraught and grieving. It is, as though your set ways begin to block any notion of believing something can save you.

I asked Judy to keep an open mind and she did. During our first meeting with Mike he answered all of our questions and had many for us too. Mike conducted a thorough analysis of our financial and health care situation, which gained him an understanding of the kind of insurances and financial assets we had in order to make the best recommendation for us. What really impressed me about Mike was his lack of judgment towards us. He was very compassionate and understanding as we explained our situation.

For my own peace of mind I needed to make sure Judy could stay in our home, with the removal of having to pay the mortgage each month. In addition, I wanted to make sure she could pay all of our bills and have the collection calls stop. Once Mike recommended a reverse mortgage and outlined, in detail, how it would meet both of my objectives, Judy and I were on board. We wanted to proceed as quickly as possible. The reverse mortgage would eliminate the $1,500 monthly mortgage payment and leave money left over in a line of credit, so future property taxes could be paid. It would also pay off all of the past due debts. This was a huge relief to us! Mike was even able to help Judy reduce her Medicare insurance costs, which was a benefit we did not expect.

The very next day we called to schedule our HUD counseling appointment and Thursday of the same week, we had our home appraised. Less than thirty days later we closed on our reverse mortgage. If it were not for Judy and me attending Mike Mertel's seminar, we realistically would have had to foreclose on our home while trying to cope with a terminal illness.

Shortly after their reverse mortgage closed, Judy's husband passed away. From time to time, Mike calls Judy to see if he can be of further assistance. Judy appreciates his thoughtfulness and will never forget how much Mike helped them in their time of need. She refers as many friends as she can to Mike, even those who might be skeptical, as she once was. Judy knows that Mike will always do what is in the best interest of his client.

About Mike Mertel, CSA

Senior Solutions
Telephone: 816-509-4880
mikemertel@kc.rr.com

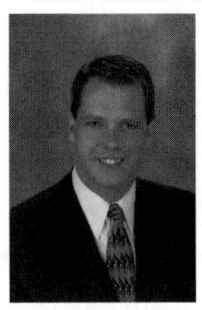

My passion is helping people, personally and professionally. Being a Certified Senior Advisor & Senior Marketing Specialist allows me the opportunity to help my clients enjoy their retirement. I provide strategies that help my clients develop financial stewardship and independence. By working together we at Senior Solutions help protect your dignity should a health issue occur and protect your family's estate and future. I only recommend a course of action to my clients that I would personally follow given the same situation. My desire is to allow you to enjoy life and pursue your passions without worrying about your current and future financial picture.

Mike is a husband and father of three children. He is a former military officer and decorated combat veteran. He and his wife are active with their church leadership and regularly volunteer to help veterans and with community organizations to help people in need.

Chapter

4

David Gardner
Advent Financial, Inc.

A BETTER LIFE FOR MY WIFE, ELIZABETH

(Story told by the Senior Client)

When I first met Dave Gardner back in 1988, he was the insurance agent for my employer. He became our financial advisor a few years later when my wife and I asked him to help us plan for our personal insurance and retirement needs. Dave worked with us in projecting how much money we would have for our retirement. We hoped to live a good life during our golden years, even though we had waited too long to seriously start saving. I have to tell you, money was tight. But Dave worked with us to create a plan and we stuck to it. My wife Elizabeth and I had to make some choices during this long process. We learned to live frugally without many of those creature comforts one comes to rely on. Our daily lives had changed, but we knew what we were striving towards - financial security in our retirement years. We found Dave to be patient, honest, and very knowledgeable. Never would I have thought, years after we met, Dave would again be so helpful in finding a solution to our greatest challenge... providing a better life for Elizabeth.

For the past twenty years, Elizabeth and I have worked at ShadyBrook, a nursing home located in rural Southern Maryland. Elizabeth worked as the office secretary and I was the Building Superintendent. My wife had the duty to handle many of the daily administrative workings of the nursing home while I was responsible for management of the physical plant. At times, the stress was difficult to handle. It is funny how you realize there is so much more to your job than the actual description. It was my responsibility to make sure the facility was clean, safe, and that the climate was well controlled. It seems the older one gets, the more a few degrees seem to affect you. One of my tasks, not to be taken lightly, was to ensure that our building was secure from outside intruders, while at the same time making sure no residents wandered off. We each took our positions quite seriously and over the years we grew close to the wonderful people who worked and lived at ShadyBrook.

Our choice of careers had a huge impact on both Elizabeth and me. We often talked about doing whatever it took to never have to live in a nursing home ourselves.

It wasn't that it was a terrible situation or anything like that. But Elizabeth and I had already spent most of our working lives in a nursing home environment. We wanted something else in our retirement and valued our independence. This goal was the reason we were so committed to the financial plan Dave helped us develop. For the two of us, no place other than home would do in our later years. Our home was just that, our home, and we intended to live out our lives there. When Elizabeth began feeling listless, we didn't worry about it at first. Then life threw us a curve-ball... she became chronically ill.

We had our plan, but, as it goes with all of our lives, ours had now changed and we were again unsure of how to go about handling our new situation. How do you cope when the love of your life becomes sick? I had to do everything in my power to make sure my wife was comfortable and as happy as possible. Before long, the challenges began to mount. Our tight budget did not last long when we lost Elizabeth's income. Even with insurance, her care costs began to mount. I have to admit there were times when I didn't know where to turn.

The illness affected her cognitive skills as well as her mobility. In order to keep our promise to live in our home, we needed to make some major structural changes. Our home was definitely not "senior friendly" and with Elizabeth growing increasingly impaired, she began using a wheelchair. This meant other changes were needed, and fast. First, we needed to build a ramp to allow Elizabeth to get in and out of the house easily. Second, a custom shower needed to be installed which would allow for access and privacy. Finally, I wanted to make improvements to our large backyard; Elizabeth loved to be outside. I wanted a secure fence for our yard, plus improve the landscape and gardens and add a fountain.

My carpentry skills would help save on labor costs but it was difficult finding the time. I still had to maintain my full-time job at ShadyBrook, not to mention the cost of material. My last resort would be my IRA. I did not want to tap into that money, because I still had a few years until retirement. I needed help and I called Dave Gardner. I explained our situation and Dave had great advice. He asked me not to make any decisions until I completed the plans for the renovations. Dave suggested I add up all my costs and estimates to really understand what would be needed financially to complete all of these improvements.

Dave was teaching insurance classes for the Life Underwriter Training Council in Bethesda, MD when I contacted him again. The classes were geared towards other insurance agents and it was during a new class called "Planning for Seniors" where Dave had to dig in and learn more about reverse mortgages. While Dave was preparing the curriculum it occurred to him that a reverse mortgage might be the answer for Elizabeth and me.

I have to admit, when Dave talked about the idea, I had no clue what a reverse mortgage was or how it worked. Dave went on to explain and I became quite intrigued by what I was hearing. I made the decision to go ahead and at least explore this avenue further. At this time Dave was not in the mortgage business and he advised me to contact Advent Financial. Dave had known the owner and was a customer himself on his own conventional mortgage. He knew

Advent to be a reputable company. I trusted Dave implicitly and without hesitation I took his advice and made the phone call.

With Dave acting as our conduit, I met with a professional from Advent Financial and was astonished at what I learned at that first meeting. If I acted on the reverse mortgage program, it would allow me to retire early from my stressful job, complete the needed renovations to the house, plus have enough left to hire a part-time caregiver in our home. We also paid off a remaining mortgage and other debt, which eliminated over $1200.00 in monthly expenses. We were able to preserve our IRA accounts. In short, the reverse mortgage would meet all our financial challenges, plus give us a bit of surplus for emergencies. Armed with this information, I quickly gave the green light and we closed on the loan soon thereafter. We were overcome with joy knowing that we kept our promise to each other to live in our home as long as possible.

Dave was so pleased with how the reverse mortgage literally changed our lives that he decided to make a new choice of his own. Four years after our reverse mortgage, Dave joined Advent as a loan officer and eventually helped us refinance our original reverse mortgage. In the process, we were able to add an additional $40,000.00 to our credit line, where it is still growing as our financial cushion.

Without Dave, I do not know how I would have been able to make a better life for Elizabeth. Today, Dave works for Advent Financial, helping those with stories similar to my own. I can tell you first hand, Dave does not view his profession in terms of policies, investments and mortgages. For him, it's about helping others and witnessing the benefits from the assistance he can offer. I could not thank Dave enough nor could I say thank you enough to Advent Financial. I think it must be pretty unusual to have somebody you can talk to who can understand so much of your financial picture. I had talked to other financial people before, but none like Dave. Dave Gardner, you are a real blessing.

About David Gardner

Advent Financial, Inc.
(410) 803-8900
www.adventmoney.com

Dave Gardner lives in Crofton, MD and specializes in senior financial issues. He is a mortgage originator and producer-manager affiliated with Advent Financial, Inc. in Bel Air, MD . He has nearly 30 years experience in financial services, including an extensive background in life and health insurance. Dave is a consultant to area banks on the reverse mortgage program and has taught Continuing Education classes to other professionals on senior topics, including retirement planning, long-term care and reverse mortgages.

Dave can be reached at (301) 221-9931 or call Advent Financial, Inc. at (410) 803-8900. You are also invited to visit the Advent website at www.adventmoney.com.

Chapter

5

Mark Yesh
Colonial Mortgage Corporation

I DON'T HAVE TO STRUGGLE ANYMORE

(Story told by the Senior Client)

My name is Thelma and I grew up in the south. Despite having lived in Michigan for more than twenty years, I am a country gal at heart. I still miss the warm southern breezes, grits, and sweet tea.

This year will come to mark my eightieth birthday and I had always heard how life could pass you by if you aren't looking. To me, there has never been a truer statement made. It seemed only yesterday that my children were young and I worked replacing vinyl seats for restaurants, hotels, and hospitals. This was hard work, especially on my back and hands. For hours, I hunched over a stool or chair patching and sewing until the seat looked just right. I took pride in my work and was interested in making sure each detail was just right. I'm reminded of my years of labor each time the weather gets cold and damp because my arthritic hands begin to ache. Holding down that job while raising my children and taking care of a home wasn't always easy. We focused on our blessings and managed to get through.

I am thankful my parents instilled good southern values in me and because of this; I take my responsibilities and promises very seriously. That's probably why I was so terribly nervous about how I was going to pay the bills since my husband passed away. Paying $550 for my monthly mortgage was almost half of the $1,200 I had to live on each month. I was tired of 'robbing Peter to pay Paul,' just to make the mortgage payment. Until I could find a better solution, this was just the way I lived. I had already thought of selling the house, ultimately I decided I wanted to stay. Selling would affect not only me but also my family. My daughter and grandson moved in with me a few years ago and I wouldn't accept money from her for rent. If I sold the house, where would we live? My daughter lived here all year round and my grandson joined us when he was home from school. I even looked into getting a home equity loan but the bank told me I didn't have enough income or credit to get approved. I was determined there was no way I was going to lose my home. I would just have to go without, before I would fall behind on my mortgage payments and get myself further into debt. I dreamed of a time when I could go to the grocery store and not price shop for every item! After all, a woman who worked hard her entire life shouldn't have to pinch pennies when she's about to turn eighty – should she?

I spent a few days each week at the local senior center and it was one of my favorite places. Everyone was always so pleasant and interesting and I loved to hear the other seniors tell stories of where they traveled or how their families were getting on. I looked forward to the needlepoint circle and despite my arthritis, attended it faithfully. I also looked forward to reading the bulletin board because there was always good information geared towards seniors that was pre-screened by the center staff before it was posted. Because I trusted the staff, a poster I saw tacked up right in the middle of that bulletin board intrigued me. The poster had a photo of a nice looking young man named Mark Yesh from Colonial Mortgage who talked about reverse mortgages. He must have an important job because his title was "VP of Reverse Mortgages". As I continued to read, I discovered in addition to originating reverse mortgages, he also trained others. This young man's information looked impressive, however I didn't know a thing about reverse mortgages and unfortunately, I was going to be late for my needlepoint circle. I needed to get moving if I was going to make it on time!

A few weeks later, would you believe I received a letter in the mail from the very same man that had his poster pinned up on the bulletin board in the senior center? The letter described a reverse mortgage as a way to eliminate a mortgage payment and get out of debt. That bit of information coupled with the information I already read about him was interesting to me. I called Mark Yesh later that same day. I wanted to learn more about reverse mortgages and if one could help my situation.

Mark Yesh, VP of Reverse Mortgages, personally answered the telephone. I thought that was a good sign. After I introduced myself, I told him that I first saw his poster on the bulletin board at the senior center and most recently received a letter from him. I asked if he would explain reverse mortgages to me. During that telephone conversation, Mark answered all of my questions and began to ask me a series of his own. He suggested we meet in person to discuss my needs further. Mark explained how he believes in fulfilling the needs of his senior clients versus selling a reverse mortgage to them. Mark's philosophy was that a reverse mortgage was not a solution for everyone and he would need a lot more information from me before he could determine if it was right for me. He wanted to discuss my needs? He cared about how I felt and my quality of life? Wow, this was amazing! I was genuinely surprised. I didn't hear those things from the bank, which turned me down for the loan or from the realtor I spoke to about selling my house. I agreed to the meeting. Maybe this really was my way out of debt after all.

As I baked cookies for my meeting with Mark, I realized how just nervous I really was. I was unsure of what to do. Just as he explained on the telephone, during our meeting, Mark outlined the ins and outs of a reverse mortgage. He asked me numerous questions about my finances. After a bit of calculating, Mark determined a reverse mortgage would be of benefit to me. He explained, in simple terms, how a reverse mortgage could change my life for the better. A reverse mortgage would eliminate my mortgage payment forever. It would also allow me to pay off additional debt. I couldn't believe how relieved I was! I could stay in my home without paying a monthly mortgage payment. There would be no more worries about how to pay my bills. I could live the rest of my life out without 'robbing Peter to pay Paul' – it was amazing! This was the solution I was searching for and made the decision to move forward.

After my reverse mortgage loan closed, I made an announcement. From that day forward, I would make a point to tell as many seniors as possible about how a reverse mortgage changed my life for the better and how wonderful Mark Yesh from Colonial Mortgage was. I'm happy to report that I have referred at least six of my senior friends to Mark. He helped each of them as much as he helped me. This reverse mortgage is the best eightieth birthday present I could have ever asked for!

About Mark Yesh, VP of Reverse Mortgage

Colonial Mortgage Corporation
Livonia, Michigan
1-800-260-5484
myesh@colonial-mortgage-corp.com
yeshucan@yahoo.com

With over eleven years of experience in the mortgage industry, since April of 2004, Mark has dedicated his time solely to reverse mortgages. He has trained and developed a team of Reverse Mortgage Specialists who consistently help over two-hundred fifty seniors each year. Mark continues to originate reverse mortgage loans for seniors in the Detroit-metro area. In addition to training Reverse Mortgage Specialists, Mark has given dozens of seminars on the topic of Reverse Mortgages. He believes in "HELPING SENIOR HOMEOWNERS ENJOY LIFE"

Chapter

6

Sam Collins
Delaware Financial Capital Corp.

SENIOR COUPLE FIND MORE HIDDEN CASH

(Story told by Sam Collins, Reverse Mortgage Professional)

As most of us know, the cost of living – medical expenses, food, fuel, taxes and insurance - continues to rise. The constant increase to the basic cost of living is especially tough for retired senior home-owners who most often rely on a fixed income.

To stay in touch with our previous clients, I write a monthly newsletter. This newsletter keeps my past clients informed, and each issue is full of tips, information and updates concerning issues impor-tant to our mature clients. One of my newsletters contained an article about a rather significant increase in the national FHA housing lending limits on reverse mortgages. Effective November 6, 2008,

HUD pronounced Section 214 of the National Housing Act, which permits new Home Equity Conversion Mortgage (HECM) national reverse mortgage limits to be raised to $417,000. This change effectively raised the mortgage limit in almost all areas across the US, and the limit is even higher in some areas. The increase in the national loan limit created a most needed opportunity for many of our Delaware senior clients.

This new national reverse mortgage limit was a significant change for the state of Delaware. There are only three counties in Delaware, and the lending limits in the past had not kept pace with the increases in home values. The Housing Economic and Recovery legislation brought new hope for many of our current clients whose home values exceeded the old county loan limits. This new loan limit now enabled many of our clients, both past and present, to utilize more of their home's equity. Our own Delaware Senator, Thomas Carper, was a strong proponent of the legislation and worked tirelessly for its passage.

I knew many of my previous clients may have had a need to utilize the new national loan limit. I received a call from Mr. and Mrs. Bierman after they learned about the new higher loan limits information. Mr. Bierman proceeded to tell me that most all of the proceeds from their previous reverse mortgage had been exhausted. He wanted to know if he could refinance and utilize more of his home's equity to take advantage of the new lending limits and some of the other benefits of the new Housing Economic and Recovery Act.

Mr. and Mrs. Bierman both received Social Security, and Mr. Bierman was retired from the DuPont Company and received a pension. Mr. Bierman said, "I feel blessed that I have not only a retirement income but my medical plan from Dupont has helped make things a lot more affordable, yet I still pay a monthly medical supplement, and having a cushion would certainly ease my mind."

When I visited Mr. and Mrs. Bierman in their home, they told me their current reverse mortgage line of credit was almost gone. Increases in cost of living expenses and some other unexpected expenses had depleted most of their savings. But with the new loan limits and the ability to refinance their current reverse mortgage using the higher lending limits was the answer. They were able to replenish their line of credit reserves.

Our reverse mortgage calculator allowed us to work out a loan scenario using the new loan limits and we discovered there was a considerable amount of unused equity that could now be utilized. Combining the new higher loan limits and lower interest rates, Mr. and Mrs. Bierman were in a position to use more equity from their home and turn that equity into a cash reserve asset. Mr. Bierman said the driving force for his new reverse mortgage was to give their family a financial cushion, and this cushion gave both Mr. and Mrs. Bierman a safe and secure feeling they had been close to losing.

When considering a reverse mortgage refinance it is important to be sure it makes both dollars and sense for the client. We recommend our homeowner's get HUD counseling again and consult with their financial advisor again to make sure they fully understand the HECM process, even if they have gone through the reverse mortgage procedure in the past. We want to ensure our senior clients are fully informed. The reverse mortgage guidelines and requirements change often, but to guarantee the best interests of our clients, we recommend receiving new HUD counseling for all refinances.

A cash infusion of several thousand dollars can be a real benefit to a senior borrower, especially at a time when IRA's, pensions, investments and 401ks have been decimated by current economic conditions.

The new Housing Economic and Recovery Act has several other advantages which helped to make the new refinance for Mr. and Mrs. Beirman's situation beneficial. One important change in the Housing Economic and Recovery Act was lenders have been capped or limited on what they can charge to originate a HECM reverse mortgage. The new origination fee cap is 2 percent of the first $200,000 and 1 percent of the amount over $200,000, with a capping of fees not to exceed $6,000. If the Housing Economic and Recovery act had not been enacted, the fees could have risen to well over $8,000. Lowering the origination fees helps reduce the closing cost. When you combine the lower origination fees and the reduced FHA mortgage insurance premium, our senior borrowers, Mr. and Mrs. Bierman, were able to put more money in their pockets.

Mr. and Mrs. Bierman have been married for 45 years and have three children. The Bierman's met in Washington, DC. . Mrs. Bierman was working for Goodyear, Mr. Bierman was a naval officer, and they both ended up working on the same government project. They were both raised as orphans, and when they met, they felt an immediate connection. Mrs. Bierman said, "I feel the secret for our longevity and success is by maintaining a positive attitude and by knowing how blessed we are for what we have."

Mrs. Bierman's words are great ones to live by, and the two of them are shining examples of how admirable our senior clients truly are.

About Sam Collins

1-877-266-9500
www.reversemortagesforyou.com
www.seniorsrighttoknow.com

Sam Collins is the President of Delaware Financial Capital Corp, a licensed mortgage banker, specializing in the reverse mortgage business and is committed to improving the lives of seniors. Sam has owned his own businesses for over 38 years and is considered a reverse mortgage industry leader and advocates to always do the right thing for his senior clients. Sam has four children and makes his home in Delaware. Contact Sam scollins@delawarefinancial.com or call 800-242-5085 for his Free report and DVD, "Ins and Outs of a Reverse Mortgage."

Chapter

7

Amy Catling, CSA
GIA Mortgage Corporation

A WIN-WIN RELATIONSHIP

(Story told by the Reverse Mortgage Professional)

Just a few short years ago nobody was talking about reverse mortgages. Not even my father and brother who were co-owners of GIA Mortgage Corporation. In those days they specialized in traditional or "forward" mortgages. After making the decision to join the family business, I had to convince both of them I wanted to get into the mortgage business in a different way. I wanted to focus on offering reverse mortgages to seniors. Convincing my family that I was serious about a career change was my very first sale – and it was a tough one! You see, my background is in bio-technology. With four small daughters at home, I wanted to pursue a career that would allow me to have a flexible schedule and help others. A focus of working with seniors would meet both of those goals. Thank goodness I was successful in making that sale. It was ironic that my first sale was to my family and not to a senior!

With my new career path mapped out, I set off to start learning as much as I could about the industry. During my training to become a loan originator is when I became aware of the concept of a reverse mortgage. The class instructors encouraged us to research and learn as much as we could about this area. With each piece of information I read, I became enamored with the benefits this financial tool could have on seniors. Admittedly, reverse mortgages are not for everyone. Closing costs are considered high for some. Additionally, someone who chooses to move forward with a reverse mortgage must really want to stay in their home for a long time. Being able to identify who a reverse mortgage was the right fit for became my passion. It was almost as if a reverse mortgage was too good to be true! I knew this was not a scam in order to take advantage of senior clients. I knew that these programs were going to be extremely helpful and I woke up each morning full of excitement, looking for people to tell.

For two years I went out and spread the word that reverse mortgages were worthwhile and not at all like the stigma associated with them. I began telling people everywhere I went, whether it was a coffee shop, a restaurant, or the grocery store, there I was explaining how a reverse mortgage could help people end their financial struggles.

Eventually, I started teaching classes at the Adult Education for Reverse Mortgages. It became something I did each year at various locations in and around my town. I found that an educational setting was the best way for me to educate people as to what a reverse mortgage is and how one might qualify. It was at a class in York, Maine where I first met Lisa and her mother, Helen. Lisa is self-employed estate attorney. She was looking at a reverse mortgage as a financial solution for her parents about fifteen years ago to improve their quality of life. Unfortunately, Lisa was unable to find any institutions that could assist her parents with a reverse mortgage.

When Lisa saw my reverse mortgage class she told her mother that this was exactly what she had been searching for. With Lisa's help and her expertise in estate planning, the process of getting a reverse mortgage underway was easy to begin.

Helen (Lisa's mother) was now a widow and eighty-two years old. Life had become a bit of a struggle since her husband's passing and Helen needed to supplement her income, which consisted of social security and a pension. While Helen's situation was certainly not desperate, a reverse mortgage would greatly improve her quality of life. She would have access to funds in case of some unforeseen expenses. The money gained would also go towards keeping up the house, garden, and purchasing gifts for her grandchildren without feeling guilty for having spent the money.

I met with Helen at her home. It was a wonderful experience to get to know her. I learned she was an avid gardener and was eager to show me her beautiful flower garden and landscaped back yard.

When it was time for us to get down to business, we decided to sit in her living room. The room was full of family photos, and as I looked at her photos, Helen began to tell me funny stories about her children and grandchildren. I can tell you one thing, after listening to those stories and getting to know Helen, she is one spunky lady!

Once we started to discuss her reverse mortgage program, she seemed a bit nervous. A very important part of my job is to make my clients feel comfortable. I assured her that was normal; that this was a conversation one did not have everyday. Helping Helen has created a professional relationship between Lisa and me. We now refer clients to each other on a regular basis, and I was thrilled that I now had a resource to call upon when I had questions for my clients I was unable to answer. Most seniors can't afford additional attorney fees, and Lisa now offers all of my senior clients a free one hour consultation. During those meetings, she takes time to answer any questions people might have. Contact Lisa E. Roche, P.A. at lmach-roche@mainerr.com or 207-351-2957. Currently, Ms. Roche practices in the following states: New Hampshire, Maine, and Massachusetts.

I ask about Helen each time I speak with Lisa. She talks about how a reverse mortgage has made a huge difference for her entire family. Lisa and her siblings do not feel guilty when Helen buys Christmas presents for their children (Helen's grandchildren) or if she wants to treat everyone to dinner.

My focus on helping seniors by offering reverse mortgages has been incredibly fulfilling for me and my family. My daughters are thrilled each time I am able to participate in their school activities.

Each time I put on my 'big girl' clothes to go to work, they know I am going out to not only work but, to help others. What a wonderful lesson for four little girls to learn! My brother now runs the day to day operations of our family business, GIA Mortgage Corporation. My father is retired, enjoying his reverse mortgage, and has more time to spend with his grandchildren. Thank goodness I was successful in helping my very first senior!

About GIA Mortgage Corporation

Telephone: 207-251-0633
Amy Catling, Certified Senior Advisor

Amy believes strongly in customer service and sincerity. She is a graduate of Assumption College with a degree in Biology with a concentration in Biotechnology. After entering the workplace in 1994 she soon realized her passion for working directly with people and using her creativity to solve problems. She became a technical sales representative for a Massachusetts Biotech company and worked in the sales and marketing department until the birth of her oldest child. This is when she decided to make the area of Maine where she had summered for years with her family her permanent home.

After staying at home with her four children: Brittany, Marissa, and twins Emma and Tessa, she decided to enter the family business with her brother, Eric and father Ernest. Since she has grown up around the business (and it is "in her blood") it seemed like a natural progression. Because of this background she understands the importance of honesty, integrity, and confidentiality, while doing business in her community.

Amy's goal as an originator is to make every transaction simple and successful. In order to do this, she strives to understand her customer's wants and needs; this in turn lets her find the best solution for each individual situation. www.seacoastreversemortgage.com GIA Mortgage is licensed in ME, NH, MA, and CT.

Chapter

8

Robert A. Weber & Associates Inc.

FIND A NEED AND MEET IT

(Story told by the Reverse Mortgage Professional)

My first experience with the mortgage industry dates back to the 1950's when I helped my Great Aunt. She needed money and I remember sitting in the bank, inquiring if it was possible for them to put a blanket lien on her house and when she passed away the house would then be sold and the bank would get their money back. It was a win-win for my Great Aunt and the bank. Thankfully, the bank agreed! Unknowingly, the idea I suggested to the bank was the first reverse mortgage I had ever negotiated!

Many years later, I started Robert A. Weber & Associates, Inc. and made the decision to work with seniors in the area of reverse mortgages because there was such a big need to fill. Time and time again, I received telephone calls from seniors who were financially dependent on social security but hadn't changed their lifestyle. Unfortunately, they dug themselves deeper into debt because they were too proud to ask for help. More often than not they did not want their children to know they had gotten to the point where they were eating cracker jacks for dinner. Bottom line: As a senior, I was in the business to help other seniors.

As an active marketer, during a trade show I was participating in, a young woman asked "I'm wondering if you could help my mother?" My thirty second commercial, while extremely blunt, seemed to peak her interest. It was the approach I always used, it fit and served me well - even in my two previous careers. I always started with "How is your budget? Because you know if your budget gets too tight you need to talk to me or have your mother talk to me."

It was then the young daughter introduced herself to me and explained her mother was a retired real estate professional. Since her father passed away, it was now up to her to keep her mother and her brother, who was disabled, in the lifestyle they were accustomed to living. It seemed as though in an instant the daughter had gone from being a daughter to the head of the household; financially responsible for both her mother and her brother and the budget was indeed getting extremely tight.

In those days (1997 or 1998), I was not licensed to do FHA loans direct with HUD. Instead; I worked with Financial Freedom. I chose to work with them because thankfully, they understood seniors. As soon as I made them aware of the daughter's and mother's need, she scheduled a meeting. After their meeting, the appraisal was done and the house was worth $100,000 however; mom owed approximately $30,000. A reverse mortgage would eliminate her monthly mortgage payments, pay off the car, and paint the house. Additionally, due to the mother being in a wheelchair, it would pay for her kitchen cabinets to be lowered so she could access them. The loan would also allow for a ramp to be installed in the front of the house. Although the loan did not give mom any rainy day money, both mother and daughter were thrilled with the proposal and made the decision to move forward with the reverse mortgage.

As fate would have it, years later I had the opportunity to work with the mother and daughter once again. It was 2003 and by this time, I was a direct correspondent to HUD and the home values in the upper dessert area increased drastically. I thought of them because the mother's home was in that area. I researched comparable home values and realized that her home value increased by $170,000! Lorraine's home was now valued at $270,000.

Immediately; I thought this would give mom her rainy day money she wanted a few years ago. I called the daughter who I previously worked closely with and explained the new situation. A refinance would give mom access to $1,000 a month. She would be able to travel and have the much needed rainy day money she wanted. Unfortunately, mom had the flu and was not able to meet until she felt well.

Six or eight months passed and the daughter was still making excuses as to why mom could not meet. Clearly something else was going on. I began to think about what might be causing both of them to be hesitant. Then it hit me! Up until now, my interaction had only been with the daughter; I had not met mom face-to-face yet! Thinking back to the approach that served me well the past two decades, my response to the daughter's put off was "I don't want any more excuses; I'm meeting with you next week. What time do you want to meet with me?"

Although skeptical, mom made the decision to at least listen to me and baked a lemon chiffon pie for the meeting. As the daughter introduced me to her mother, she was surprised to see a senior gentleman standing in front of her. Mom's interest was peaked and now wanted to know everything about me. She was determined to figure out who this person was, without hesitation, mom asked me to share my resume with her. I immediately realized that she was a no nonsense kind of lady and I appreciated her approach.

It was time to get down to business. I pulled out my HB-12 calculator and started to quote information that included interest rates. Mom went to the buffet in the dining room and pulled out her HB-12 calculator to double-check my numbers. Our numbers indeed matched! She then asked why I was so persistent in contacting the daughter in order to meet. I explained one of my core philosophies, which I live by: if there is a need that I can fill for my client; it was my responsibility to fill that need.

Once mom realized that I was legitimate and the proposal I recommended made a lot of sense, she put a pot of coffee on and asked if

I wanted a slice of her home made lemon chiffon pie. Of course, I accepted and the loan papers were signed that very day.

Thanks to the outcome, the daughter feels so much more secure now that the financial pressure has been removed. She even asked, if I could assist her on a refinance for a rental property she owned. Mom was able to use her rainy day money to take various cruises and experience life in a whole new way. Overall; their quality of life has improved immensely!

About Robert A. Weber & Associates, Inc.

Telephone: 1-866-338-5767
Email: bobweberloans@hotmail.com
Robert A. Weber, President

As a senior with over twenty years of experience in both the forward and reverse sides of the industry, Bob Weber prides himself on providing proactive financial services to his clients. Bob's ability to meet his client's needs is what gets him out of bed each morning.

Contact Bob Weber for: debt consolidation, home equity loans, lowering your monthly mortgage payments, new home purchases, and of course – for a reverse mortgage.

Chapter

9

Amy and Joseph Arnone
Citizens Financial Mortgage, Inc.

OUR FAMILY GROWS WITH EACH CLIENT WE HELP

(Story told by Reverse Mortgage Professional)

Let me start by introducing myself. My name is Amy Arnone, I am a Mortgage Business owner. My partner is Joseph Arnone and he is my brother. We are partners in our branch of "Citizens Financial Mortgage," located in New York City. We have been successful business partners all of our adult life, but have been best of friends all our life. Joseph and I are 14 months apart. We share a lot of the same likenesses as well as excelling at different things but one thing we share is compassion. We incorporate this into our day to day business as well as our own personal lives. We value each other as well as our family. We extend ourselves to others in need which gives us a great sense of satisfaction. I know that we have been successful because of this. I believe the source of your individual values come from your upbringing. Joseph and I are very fortunate that we have grown up in a family full of love, inspiration, compassion and trust. Our parents, Steven and Amelia are wonderful people as well as our older brother Steven Jr. and our older sister Stephanie.

As a child, I don't remember a time when our house wasn't full of laughter and happiness. It wasn't until my early teenage years that I realized that we had our own financial issues which put a lot of stress on our parent's. I realized that owning our home wasn't something that I should take for granted. It was at this point that I asked my parent's what I could do to help. They were always humble and asked very little of us. All of the Arnone children held small jobs to help with the finances of the household. This is where we learned our work ethic. There was a time during these years that we came very close to losing our home. I can remember accompanying my parents to and from one office to another trying to find the help we needed to maintain our life. It was also at this time that I realized that the business professionals we sought advice from were only worried about their own "bottom line". Their advice was short and never did they discuss or ask about our future finances past whatever transaction they were proposing.

Although young, I realized that these were not the answers my parents were looking for. What they needed was a long term solution. Through our hard times, we grew up fast. My parent's eventually found the resources they needed and life returned to normal. But the experience stayed with me and I began to look for employment that would gratify me. I began working for mortgage companies doing anything I could and took in everything. It didn't take me long to open my own company. Yet I knew something was missing. It was my brother, Joseph. At the time he was attending college part time trying to figure out what he wanted for the rest of his life. I suggested he work with me part time and he agreed. It wasn't long after he started that we realized that he was indeed the missing piece. So together we vowed that we would bring about a company that would put the needs of its clients at the forefront and promised that we would always keep their best interest at heart!

I am proud to say that Joseph and I have gained the reputation we set out for. Our client base is mostly referral and we take pride in that. We have come to view our clients as friends. Once involved, a relationship grows. A relationship based on trust, respect and the common goal of long term security. Keeping long term goals at the forefront allow us to assess the best products for our clients.

I would like to share a story with you about a family that really impacted us. It was because of this family that we chose to avidly make seniors aware of the Reverse Mortgage.

It all started with a referral call from a realtor. The realtor asked us to speak with a family and see if we could help them. She informed us that they were at the end of their rope. She told us that she knew these people would touch our hearts and they truly did.

So later that day, we sat with this family. The daughter explained to us that her father passed some years ago. Their mother had tried to maintain their family home. It was impossible on an income that was reduced by $2000 a month after his death. The mortgage payment alone was twice as much as she made a month and the house was now in foreclosure.

After hearing that the home had been in their family for over 90 years, we knew that we had to do everything possible to keep it that way. This family has already been through so much and we made it our mission to solve their problem!

As the conversation continued we realized that a lot of what the daughter said reflected some type of mortgage industry language. I asked her if she had ever worked in the mortgage industry. She replied; "No, but the home has been in foreclosure for over three years and I have been to eight mortgage companies before coming here". "I have spent thousands of dollars on attorneys, appraisal fees and bank application fees." Unfortunately, not one person had been able to help.

You see their mother was 86 years old and in need of a guaranteed income in addition to getting this house out of foreclosure. It was obvious to us that the perfect solution was a Reverse Mortgage. When we mentioned it to her she told us that she had heard of it but didn't know the details. No one ever suggested a Reverse Mortgage to them so she didn't think it was an option. We explained further how this loan would be able to solve every financial hardship she faced. It would pay off the loan that was in foreclosure, it would payoff all of her debt, and it would produce a monthly income for her mother.

They were elated with happiness and relief! Although the loan was a tough one because of the foreclosure, we worked diligently to get the financing in place. The process was fast and easy and being that reverse mortgages do not require much paperwork, the process is virtually effortless. The qualifications for the borrower(s) are based on age, home value, county in which the property is located, and that it is the borrower's primary residence. An important factor is that income documentation is never required for any reverse mortgage. The purpose of the mortgage is to secure a guaranteed income for the rest of the senior's life!

Since our initial meeting the family has told all of their friends, family and local community members about Reverse Mortgages. They felt that they needed to share the knowledge that they now possessed with everyone that could use the help because they were so few people who were willing and able to help them.

After the loan closed, Joseph and I continued working with this family; in fact we made sure that this family sought the advice of an estate planner. The estate planner would be able to draft the correct trust so they can assure the estate would be in their family forever! We always take the extra steps to make sure our clients are protected for the future. When working with our clients we listen and asses their needs to completely fulfill all of their financial goals with experience, knowledge and know-how.

About Citizens Financial Mortgage, Inc.

1-800-738-6500
www.seniorcitizensloans.com
Amy Arnone
Joseph Arnone

Citizens Financial Mortgage loan programs financed: Conventional, Fannie Mae, Freddie Mac, FHA, VA, SONYMA, Commercial Mortgages and Reverse Mortgages.

Licensed States: AK, CA, CO, CT, DE, FL, ME, MD, MA, MN, NJ, NY, PA, VA, WY.

Customer Service is not a cliché it is our standard of commitment, which has upheld our large network of referral based business. Customer satisfaction is our goal!

We intend to be your "lender for life."

Chapter

10

Jerry Boyd
Troy Freesemann
Waterstone Mortgage Corp.

SAVING A SINKING SHIP

(Story told by the Senior Client)

Our financial pain had hit an all-time high. We were barely adrift in a deep, dark sea of debt. We were making payments of $250 each week on our mortgage plus trying to play catch up on past due taxes, and medical bills. As the dollars we owed mounted, it became impossible to pay our utility bills much less put food on the table. The thought of having to choose between shelter and food was utterly disheartening.

Bob and I were so unsure of what to do it was paralyzing! We were afraid that we might lose the house, Bob's illness worsening, and the whole uncertainty of our future. How would we explain losing our home to our family and friends?

One evening, while enjoying our favorite television show, we saw a commercial for a reverse mortgage. Bob and I agreed it sounded almost too good to be true but still made the decision to request a DVD. We wanted to learn more about reverse mortgages and see if it might help. After all, the DVD was free and that was at least in our budget!

When the DVD arrived, Bob and I watched it intently. It was full of important information, Troy and Jerry appeared like they knew what they were discussing. We were still unsure, if it even made sense to talk to them. We did not want to waste their time, with Bob's health getting worse; taking care of his medical issues became more of a priority.

While Bob and I were dealing with life, thank goodness, Troy Freesemann continued to contact us. If I remember correctly, he called several times and even sent letters to us, gentle reminders that there was a solution. Unfortunately, the timing was never quite right on our part, as it was important to me that Bob was well enough to participate in the meeting.

Time sailed by as day after day I was still completely overwhelmed by fear and worry over unpaid bills and Bob's health. The summer months came to an end and nights started to get colder. You could smell autumn in the air. I began to worry about how we were going to pay for our heating bills during the cold Midwest winter months. There were only so many blankets we could use to keep warm and I could not risk Bob getting a chill and making his sickness worse. It was time to call Troy and Jerry and take them up on their offer to meet.

Troy seemed genuinely happy to hear from me and even remembered my name which made me feel a bit more at ease. During our conversation, he told me a little bit about his company and that he and Jerry were business partners. He explained that they take pride in being able to assist people that are in difficult financial situations but might not know where to turn. Troy and Jerry have the ability to work with reverse mortgages that need a little bit more care and creativity in putting it all together to make sure everything works out successfully. He even took the time to outline how their business partnership worked. Troy's role was to prepare us for our upcoming meeting, answer our initial questions, and if we decided to move forward, he then processes all of the paperwork. Jerry's job was to meet face to face with their customers to gather all of the necessary details and recommend the right solution. Troy confessed that this division of responsibilities was the secret to their long business partnership, because they did not see much of each other! Troy went on to say something that surprised me. He extended an invitation for any of our close advisors, friends, family, or kids to participate in the upcoming consultation.

By the end of our conversation, Troy answered all of my questions and scheduled a time when his partner, Jerry Boyd, would be out to our house and meet with us. All of this seemed to make sense to me; we scheduled the appointment for the following week.

Jerry arrived at our house and Bob and I immediately knew we liked him. Instead of acting like a typical 'sales person' and jumping to the numbers, Jerry wanted to get to know us. After about an hour, Bob & I realized he seemed genuinely interested in learning about our life, our son, and how difficult the past few years had been. We could tell that he really cared about being able to help us. Also, Jerry wanted us to be sure we understood the 'why' or reason behind everything he asked us and recommended. If we could not answer his questions or were unsure of the answer, he wanted us to be honest and tell him 'I don't know the answer' but be sure to make a note and call Troy when you do have the answer. Bob and I began to trust and have confidence in what he and Troy had to offer.

After listening to our answers to a number of his questions, Jerry started to go through the details and what we could do and could not do. He was very candid, and we appreciated it. He explained that while a reverse mortgage was the best solution for us, there were going to be a few fairly large challenges to overcome. The fact that we still had a substantial balance on our existing mortgage coupled with past due taxes, we would have to come up with between $12-13,000 in order for our loan to close. Our immediate reaction was not good. We couldn't afford our weekly grocery bill – how in the world were we going to get our hands on that kind of money?

Then, Jerry asked Bob the most peculiar question. He asked Bob if the Cadillac in our garage was important to him anymore. And Bob's immediate reaction was 'I could care less if we had a Cadillac or if we had a Pinto'. Bob was clear that he didn't care about the prestige of the Cadillac anymore. He cared about being able to be comfortable. That was the answer Jerry was hoping for, that car represented a huge portion of the money that we needed to bring to the closing table. Now that we saw a way out of our sinking ship, Bob and I made the commitment to do whatever we needed to do to make this work.

The next step was for us to figure out how to sell the Cadillac. We placed an ad in the local newspaper but weren't sure if it would sell since we lived in a small town. Jerry suggested the option of selling the car at auction. He had some acquaintances in the auction business and gladly made a few introductions for us. Thankfully, we sold the car!

About Jerry Boyd and Troy Freesemann

866-800-0280
Jerry Boyd, Home Equity Advisor, CSA
(Certified Senior Advisor)
Troy Freesemann, Home Equity Advisor, CSA
(Certified Senior Advisor)
jboyd@waterstonemortgage.com
tfreesemann@waterstonemortgage.com

We have been in business for over 12 years and have specialized in Reverse Mortgages for over 3 years. Troy and Jerry are passionate about working with seniors and love educating people about the benefits of reverse mortgages. Our philosophy is: if you share information with people and have their best interest in mind, you can provide the best service and make a lot of friends along the way. When you do something that works for people and improves their quality of life, it's a good thing.

Chapter
11

Mike and Josh Borba
MLS Reverse Mortgage

WE HELPED EACH OTHER

(Story told by Reverse Mortgage Professional)

Kitty and Charlie had big dreams. Dreams of traveling the world, experiencing Paris in springtime and whale watching in Alaska. With their children grown and most of life's ups and downs behind them, they both agreed, it was time to focus on Kitty and Charlie. Living hand to mouth at this time in their life was not part of the dream. Their focus needed to shift, away from the children and grandchildren and move towards improving the quality of life they deserved.

As head of the household; it was Charlie's job to handle the finances. It was apparent that the stipend from social security they were relying on in their golden years was not going to be enough to allow them to travel the world. Being resourceful, Charlie started to research alternative solutions and realized that he was literally sitting in their solution. He saw all of the advertisements on television and received quite a bit of mail about reverse mortgages. Charlie had made up his mind to learn whatever he could about how a reverse mortgage could help them fulfill their dreams. Sadly, Charlie passed away before the research was complete. Heartbroken, traveling the world just didn't seem appealing anymore.

For months, time stood still for Kitty. Going through the motions of everyday activities took up so much energy. Everyone offered to help her but she did not want help – she wanted her husband. As the fog slowly began to lift, Kitty's close friend and next door neighbor Debra Genovia began to notice Kitty was struggling financially. Debra was in private geriatric care management (www.caremanager.org) and she had seen this type of situation too many times. One spouse passes away and the other is left to deal with so many financial burdens. Everyone thinks they have planned for situations such as this but, the reality was that no matter how much you plan – it is never easy. Debra was able to get Kitty to open up to her and share her concerns. After carefully listening to Kitty, Debra offered a solution to Kitty's problems. She suggested Kitty contact MLS Reverse Mortgage to see if they could help by way of a reverse mortgage. Debra had a personal experience with Mike and Josh Borba at MLS Reverse Mortgage as she was one of their customers and had recently refinanced her existing home loan with their help. Debra raved about how friendly and smart the father-son team was and felt certain they could help.

Kitty did remember Charlie talking about reverse mortgages and she fondly remembered how he collected all of the mailers he had received. He called each company, asked questions and took concise notes in the process. She really missed him and wished he was able to help her make this decision. Knowing that Charlie was in the process of exploring a reverse mortgage helped her to feel a bit more comfortable about the idea. Maybe now was the time for her to explore a reverse mortgage. It seemed scary to do this on her own but deep down inside she knew it was something she needed to at least investigate. Because Debra was someone she trusted, Kitty made the decision to call Mike and Josh Borba.

Before the first meeting, Kitty visited with each of her children and told them of her plans. Kitty explained that in addition to using the money to pay off bills and to travel, the house was in need of a few repairs. Her hope was that a reverse mortgage would provide the necessary funds to meet her objectives. Kitty wanted to be sure that her children were part of any decision that she made. She also wanted to be sure that her family understood the details of a reverse mortgage. Kitty and her daughter Janice prepared a list of questions and were well prepared for the meeting with MLS Reverse Mortgage.

Walking into the MLS Reverse Mortgage office, Kitty felt a twinge of excitement as she started to think about not having to hide the fact that she was living hand to mouth from her children. She knew the kids suspected things were out of sorts but she was able to shield them from everything. The past few months had been so difficult for her. With mourning her husband and staying strong for the children, she felt as though she was drowning in a sea of financial burden. As she sat and waited, Kitty's thoughts drifted to visiting her sister in Minnesota. She thought how wonderful it would be, spending time with Carolyn once again. It occurred to her that a reverse mortgage could be just the thing to help her through this troublesome time.

The meeting began with Kitty and Janice watching a short fifteen minute DVD that explained what a reverse mortgage is and how it works. It was a pleasant surprise to learn that Mike and Josh had more than twenty eight years of experience between the two of them. Janice started to ask the questions that she and her siblings had regarding the impact a reverse mortgage would have on their mother's future. Questions like: Were there any monthly payments? Does the loan accrue interest? What happened if Kitty had to leave the house and go into a nursing home? Would there be money for the repairs?

Mike and Josh took the time to answer all of their questions. They were very honest and made sure Kitty and Janice thoroughly understood each scenario. By the end of the meeting, it was apparent to everyone that a reverse mortgage was the solution that would meet Kitty's needs. After getting all of the necessary paperwork together and meeting with a HUD counselor, there was no doubt in Kitty's mind she was doing the right thing. Traveling without Charlie was not going to be the same but; she knew it was what he would want for her.

It has been almost a year since Kitty's loan closing and to this day, she is still, so very grateful to Mike and Josh for their kindness. They truly went above and beyond for her and when a contractor appeared to be taking advantage of Kitty, Mike and Josh stepped in and saved her roughly $4500.00 for termite repairs.

Kitty's independence has grown. She does not rely on her kids, as a matter of fact; her children have even commented on how her sense of security has become steadfast. Mike and Josh are not only a resource, but have also become part of her family. With an increase in advertising to seniors, Kitty receives quite a few offers in the mail to refinance her reverse mortgage. She calls upon Josh and Mike on a regular basis to discuss the offers and they help her understand the options available. In between vacations, Kitty also catches up with Mike and Josh, getting updates as to what is happening in their lives and with their families. Their business relationship has become a wonderful friendship.

It's very apparent how much this reverse mortgage has benefited Kitty's life, but what's not visible to everyone is how much this reverse mortgage impacted the lives and business model of Mike and Josh. It was such a rewarding experience working with Kitty that Mike and Josh decided to focus most of their energy on helping seniors by educating and offering reverse mortgages. Without realizing it, Kitty helped to shape the future direction of MLS Reverse Mortgage!

About MLS Reverse Mortgage

Mike and Josh Borba
13478 Luther Road, Suite C
Auburn, CA 95063
Telephone: 530-888-6000
or 1-888-888-4834
www.MLSMONEY.com
www.LearnAboutReverseMortgages.com

photo by Shirley Borba

Mike Borba started working in the Real Estate industry in 1979. Formally a chemist for Sunkist Growers, Mike became a Broker in 1986 and started in the lending business in 1992. Mike's successful and ethical business practices have produced many happy and repeat clients.

Josh Borba graduated from San Francisco State University in 2002 with a degree in Business Administration and an emphasis on International Business. After graduation, Josh spent a few months in Spain, studying Spanish before returning home to open MLS Mortgage with his father, Mike Borba. Josh recently married his college sweetheart, Alexis.

Chapter

12

Ryan Neuman
Cornerstone Reverse Mortgage

A MODEST SUCCESS

(Story told by the Reverse Mortgage Professional)

Ken and Dorothy instantly struck me as the quintessential senior couple. Two people who have spent their lives together, understanding that they both have the responsibility to take care of one another. At this stage in their life, it was Ken who had become the primary caregiver for Dorothy. With age came some of the all too familiar medical issues which most of us will eventually face. For Ken, his only thoughts centered on caring for his loving wife.

Living in a home built just after World War II, Ken and Dorothy enjoyed a wonderfully modest life in the Sonoma region of northern California. It was their wish to maintain this lifestyle, one that they

67

loved, well into their golden years. As Dorothy's condition progressed, the medical bills began to escalate. Not only were the medical
bills daunting, there was also the maintenance of the home which
needed financial attention. Over the years they had borrowed money
against their home and they were beginning to feel the monthly
tightening on their budget.

When I first met them, I quickly surveyed the situation and realized that Ken would be the one to absorb and process most of the
information regarding this transaction. I realized that even in Dorothy's diminished capacity, Ken was going to make sure that his wife
was part of the entire process.

Ken and Dorothy first learned about Cornerstone Reverse Mortgage from an ad on television. We had been using a local veteran
personality as our spokesperson and Ken had responded after seeing
a few of the spots. It became clear to Ken and Dorothy that they
needed to do something and from what they heard on the television,
it was just enough to peak their interest and make the call.

It is sometimes amazing what I remember after meeting clients a
few times. I remember how Dorothy was fixated on baseball and how
she loved her Oakland A's. We had some spirited conversations, you
see, I am a life-long Giants fan. I also remember Ken being a veteran,
serving his country for 25 years and being part of the Korean conflict.
Reasons like these are why our seniors should not have to struggle
financially during their retirement. Ken and Dorothy were prepared
but just needed that extra help which would come in the form of a
reverse mortgage.

From the outset it was clear that they had medical bills which needed immediate attention. In addition to that, the roof was in much need of repairs, having gone many years without any maintenance and it was clearly evident from the water damage that their home had suffered. The water had not only damaged the roof but also a few bedrooms, ceilings, and walls. Ken and Dorothy were both exacerbated by the situation and how it came to be. It was simple; there simply was not enough money to go around.

The main reason why this was going to work well for them and for this whole process was due to our level of communication. I was able to show Ken and Dorothy that I was there to act as a resource for them. Not to sell them a product but to give them the information they needed to make the best decision. It became quite obvious that they needed to make one of the biggest decisions of their life, one that would benefit them for years to come. I firmly believe that my experience with seniors and the way in which I communicate is the top reason why Cornerstone has been so successful. For most seniors, they are not in a situation where they have advisors, someone who can represent them through a process like a reverse mortgage. With that being the case, I rely tremendously on the way I put the process in a language that people can understand. I try to tone down the presentation so that it is not too analytical or financial, so it becomes something which my senior clients can understand and manage.

Ken and Dorothy did become comfortable with me and it showed throughout the entire process. They were able to make decisions based on the information I provided and at no time did they feel forced or pushed into a situation. After spending twenty years in their home, I did not think that neither Ken nor Dorothy had any ideas about living elsewhere.

About sixty days after we had first met, the reverse mortgage that we worked on closed. Prior to the closing, Ken and Dorothy had a mortgage payment of approximately $1,000.00 per month. With the reverse mortgage this payment went away. It is always a joy when people discover that such a payment has disappeared. Furthermore, a lump sum of $30,000.00 was paid out. This money went to Dorothy's medical bills and for the required work for the house. I was able to enlist a contractor that I have used many times for my clients and myself. (A nice gentleman who understands senior clients and is able to put them at ease, even with major work projects.) Under his leadership, the roof and all of the other ancillary repairs were done and the house is in great shape once again.

The final piece of the reverse mortgage came in the form of a ten-year payment plan. Ken and Dorothy opted to receive a monthly payment of $900.00. This money could be used for any financial need that they might have, from groceries to medical bills, or fulfilling some dream, which they may have. Amazingly, Ken and Dorothy realized they had just undergone a $1,900.00 monthly swing, plus $25,000.00 per year in newfound income.

I must say that I was quite impressed with the way in which Ken and Dorothy handled the entire process. Think about it, there was a constant flow of information being communicated between the client, the lending institution, the contractors, and myself. Not once did I ever sense any level of frustration coming from Ken and Dorothy. I remember their relief at the closing, knowing that they would never have to worry about their finances any longer.

As I observed their transformation, I was once again reminded why my career with Cornerstone Reverse Mortgage has been such a rewarding experience. Sometimes you have people who will literally jump up and down with excitement at the closing or you will have people like Ken and Dorothy who let you know in a silent and comforting way that you have just given them the best possible gift.

It has been a few years since they had their reverse mortgage and I am happy to say that all is well. I saw Ken and Dorothy a few months ago and it was evident that they were still enjoying the effects from their reverse mortgage.

About Ryan Neuman

2544 Cleveland Ave, Suite 110
Santa Rosa, CA 95403
Toll Free: (800) 493-7098
Office: (707) 578-7098
r_neuman@msn.com
www.cornerstonereverse.com

Ryan Neuman and Cornerstone Reverse Mortgage expertise helps create lifetime income, allowing people to live their lives to the fullest. Ryan's goal is to offer each individual a tailored solution that best meets his or her life needs. Ryan has a long history of helping people with 15 years of Real Estate and Mortgage expertise. Ryan partners with his wife Sheri who is a Certified Public Accountant, along with Ryan's finance background they bring 30 years of understanding to your picture to help bring about the right choices for you.

Chapter

13

Robert O. Brown
Delaware Financial Capital Corp.

A GOOD NEIGHBOR

(Story told by the Senior Client's Neighbor)

Have you ever met a person who was so nice and so giving, that it was easy for someone to take advantage of them? I live across the street from the nicest lady in the world and unfortunately, she couldn't say 'no' to anyone, which is how she got into this terrible predicament.

Friends, family members, and even neighbors would ask Annie (Senior Client) for help paying their bills. Annie always gave and gave without thinking about herself and ignoring her own bills. She went without so that others could have what they needed. Annie used a series of refinances to get quick cash which got her further and further into debt. She would do one refinance and realized she couldn't afford that one then do another and another. That's when I stepped in. Enough was enough! Someone, even if it was her neighbor, had to stop this vicious cycle and be an advocate for Annie.

I could relate with Annie's financial situation. A few years ago, I was having problems making ends meet. I don't think anyone realizes how difficult it is to live on a fixed income until they actually have to. Anyway, I worked with Robert Brown at Delaware Financial who helped me get a reverse mortgage. Robert was honest, dependable, and made sure I understood everything about my reverse mortgage loan. Since my mortgage payments were eliminated and I had a nest egg to tap into when I needed it, my life had changed drastically. It is amazing how you can enjoy life so much more when financial stress is removed from your life. I really got lucky when I met and worked with Robert Brown. It is a blessing that he and his partners at Delaware Financial take their responsibilities as seriously as they do. Robert is one of those guys that 'walks his talk'. He is a true advocate for his senior clients. I knew Annie needed Robert's help and intended to make sure she got it.

It was a sunny May afternoon in Baltimore, Maryland. It was one of those days that you wanted to spend wandering around the Inner Harbor – warm but, not so warm that your ice cream cone would melt too fast. I enjoyed things so much more now that I had my reverse mortgage and knew Annie would too. It was on that beautiful spring day when Robert first met with Annie. Annie was very nervous and anxious; after all, this wasn't the first mortgage person she had met with. Her experiences weren't the best to say the least. But, Robert's pleasant and calm demeanor put her at ease. After review of the current situation, Robert told Annie the good news - the reverse mortgage would completely pay off her mortgage! Annie was thrilled with the news. Annie's loan was cleared to close a few weeks later and Robert called her to schedule her loan closing appointment. Much to our surprise, Annie never returned Robert's telephone calls.

Do you remember when I mentioned that Annie was the nicest person in the world? Well, would you believe that Annie was working with another mortgage person the entire time she was working with Robert? It turns out the other mortgage person was a friend of a friend. While Annie felt guilty about not working with Robert, she felt worse not helping out her friends. The worst part was other company steered her towards a loan that even at the smallest payment level she couldn't afford. Annie was stuck in a far worse situation than before she signed those loan papers. There was absolutely no way she could afford that payment.

Despite Annie's lack of response, Robert was persistent about staying in contact. He sent her letters to remind her that he was there for her should she need his services. Robert was persistent because he knew that if Annie continued to refinance her mortgage loan she would eventually lose her home.

Time flew by as it always does and the Christmas season was upon us. Annie and I were sitting in my kitchen catching up over a cup of coffee. During that conversation, she confided in me that the refinance loan she had signed months prior was the straw that broke the camel's back. She had been unable to make her mortgage payments and received a notice from the mortgage company that her home was now in foreclosure. The realization that she was going to lose her home was horrible. At 72 years old, she was going to be homeless. Annie was an emotional wreck. She needed help and didn't know where to turn. I knew the answer to her problem – it was Robert Brown at Delaware Financial.

Annie was hesitant about calling Robert. After all, she didn't return his telephone calls and felt guilty about the way she treated him. I told her not to worry as I dialed Robert's telephone number. Once I had him on the line, I gave him a brief update about Annie's situation then handed her the telephone.

Much to Annie's surprise, Robert was not judgmental towards her at all. He told her not to worry about anything that had been done. It was the past and couldn't be changed. Robert made sure that Annie understood he could still help her and quickly. To prove he was serious, by the end of their conversation, Robert had the appraisal set up for December 21st, a few short days from then.

Eighteen days later, Annie sat across the table from Robert at her loan closing meeting. She was ecstatic! Annie's home was saved from foreclosure and she would never have a mortgage payment to worry about again. As tears streamed down her face, Annie told Robert how grateful she was for his help, patience, and understanding.

I am so happy that I introduced Annie to Robert. Since her loan closing with Delaware Financial, she is a new person! I noticed her nephew carrying paint and supplies into her house the other day. I guess she'll finally get to give herself a nice gift instead of giving something to everyone else.

About Robert O. Brown

Delaware Financial Capital Corp.
Telephone: 1-877-435-3388
Email: rbrown@delawarefinancial.com
www.defcc.com

Robert Brown has been in the mortgage business for over sixteen years and has been helping seniors with various tax and financial advice since he earned his CPA certificate in 1984. Robert's philosophy in dealing with his clients is to go the extra mile to make sure they have the best financial loan choices. Delaware Financial Capital Corp. is licensed by PA Department of Banking; Licensed Mortgage Banker in Delaware and Maryland.

Chapter

14

Meg Twohey
Freedom Capital Reverse

NEW POSSIBILITIES

(Story told by the Senior Client's Daughter)

"I will never forget this moment," I thought to myself. This was the very first time in my thirty-four years that I witnessed my mother as a person and not as a parent. I sat across the table from her and it occurred to me that at age 76, her thoughts and decisions had never caught up with her age. My entire life, my sister and I had known her as a hardworking, intelligent, and caring person. She was a force to be reckoned with and extremely determined when she had her mind set on something. Even today, despite having medical issues, she still drives several miles each and every day to the other end of the county she lives in to teach. My mom is so passionate about molding and shaping the young minds in her classroom. Until the loan-closing meeting, she planned on continuing to teach indefinitely, health issues would never stop my mom from teaching. I had learned so much about my mother throughout this entire process. I learned that she wanted to travel and had a desire to own a business. To be perfectly honest, up until this moment, it never occurred to me that she had unfulfilled dreams. I could see a new sparkle in her eyes. Things were about to change and I was so grateful to Meg for introducing new possibilities to our family. But wait, I am jumping so far ahead of myself. Let me explain how it all began.

My mother wanted to refinance her house and rental property. Both homes had adjustable rate mortgages with negative amortization and she was concerned about the constant increases in her monthly payments because she was on a fixed income. My mother's original goal was to obtain fixed rate loans for both properties and get cash out for some repairs. As I previously mentioned, my mom had physical challenges and yet still worked full time as a college professor. It would be devastating, financially, if she had to stop working. She had medical costs due to health issues the previous year and needed to plan for any unforeseen future medical needs. She wanted to make some repairs to her home and needed money for that. We asked our family accountant for advice and he referred us to Meg Twohey at Freedom Capital Reverse.

From the beginning, we were participating in what I now know is termed an 'expansive discovery process'. In retrospect, my mother and I thought we would meet with Meg and she would do exactly what we asked, which was for her to refinance both mortgages. Thankfully, I am forever grateful she took another approach! Meg began our meeting by asking my mother an infinite amount of questions about what was next for her in the second chapter of her life. I wondered why Meg kept asking questions such as "when you aren't working, how do you like to spend your time" or "if you were not dependent on your current paycheck, how would that change your life?" During the conversation, dreaming aloud, Meg even suggested my mom take a trip to Europe. Mom was so perplexed by the idea admitting that she had never thought it was possible. The process helped my mom articulate her life aspirations versus having a discussion framed by a mortgage.

After reviewing all of our options, Meg came to the conclusion that a reverse mortgage for the primary residence and a traditional refinance for the rental property would be the best solution. With mom living on a fixed income, a reverse mortgage made perfect sense. A reverse mortgage would enable mom to improve her cash flow by $1,800 per month and give her access to $50,000 for property repairs and to pay off medical bills. Best of all, a reverse mortgage gave mom access to a substantial line of credit that she could access at any time, as needed, for any use without a monthly payment.

Before solutions were presented to my mom, Meg called me to discuss the option of a reverse mortgage. I guess Meg picked up on the fact that my mom has a very strong personality and was unsure of how she would feel about a reverse mortgage. There was only one small problem. My mom was dead set against a reverse mortgage.

She heard from someone (unable to remember who it was) that you can lose your home, or that you do not retain the title to the home. We now know that both of those ideas are completely untrue. However; at that point in the process, she had her own ideas of how to "fix" her financial situation and trust me; a reverse mortgage was not high on her list.

The more Meg and I discussed the option of a reverse mortgage for Mom's primary residence, the more I embraced the idea. It really did make perfect sense. I wanted to do some homework of my own before I approached my mom with this idea. I called the tax preparer that referred us to Freedom Capital as well as Mom's Estate Attorney.

After a review of the proposal, both agreed it was the best solution. By the end of those conversations, there was not a doubt in my mind that my mom should proceed with Meg's proposed plan. I just needed to convince her!

When I first discussed Meg's solution with my mother, it was a fairly short conversation. She wanted absolutely nothing to do with the idea of a reverse mortgage. Mom had heard bad things about them and unfortunately, believed all of those bad things to be true. I knew I had to find a way to get my mother to listen to me. I knew a reverse mortgage for her primary residence was the best approach. I made the decision to do whatever I could to get my mom to at least hear me out. I was a woman on a mission – determined and stubborn. I was going to give my mother a run for her money, after all – I learned the art of persistence from the master herself!

Eventually, my mother realized the solution that Freedom Capital proposed, provided more than she ever imagined. She was expecting a "traditional" mortgage solution and she came away with a lifestyle solution. Her needs were so much different than she originally thought. The reverse mortgage offered solutions to all of her needs now and in the future. By eliminating mom's mortgage payment and improving her monthly cash flow, it would allow her to stop working if necessary. It would also provide access to additional money for medical costs, property improvements, and personal desires such as travel.

My sister and I are thrilled about the experience my mom had with Freedom Capital. Because of Meg Twohey's expertise, there is less emotional and financial burden for both of us. Unknowingly, Meg had given to us a priceless gift. She introduced us to a part of our mother we had never known. My mother...a woman, teacher, and future business owner.

About Meg Twohey
(619) 850-7065 Cell

Freedom Capital Reverse specializes in asset optimization through strategic equity planning. We feel that a thoughtful, purposeful plan transcends individual financial tools. As such, our company integrates financial and mortgage planning strategies to ensure the best results for our clients. Whether our clients are just starting their careers, planning for retirement or currently living in retirement, we address their specific financial needs and goals and apply appropriate solutions. We believe that when used properly, home equity can be put to work to provide financial security through all stages of life. Freedom Capital Reverse is licensed in the state of California. Visit: www.freedomcap.com.

Freedom Capital Reverse is no longer in business. Meg Twohey is now a Wells Fargo Home Mortgage Consultant and can be reached at 619-850-7056

Chapter

15

Jennifer Hart, CSA

AN ADVOCATE FOR ALICE

(Story told by the Reverse Mortgage Professional)

Absolutely nothing in my twenty-five years of combined real estate and mortgage industry experience could have prepared me for this emotionally charged situation. The story I am about to share is one that is often untold because of how raw and uncomfortable the circumstance. I am proud to say that under frustrating circumstances, I stayed true to myself as a person and a reverse mortgage professional and was an advocate for someone who had no one else to turn to - - my senior client, Alice.

It all started with a telephone call I had received from Alice's local banker, Tom. He was a no-nonsense kind of guy - - direct and to the point. "I have a lady in her 70's who is being kicked out of her house in three weeks. What can you do?" asked Tom. After asking a few preliminary questions, I asked Tom to arrange for a meeting with Alice and myself - - the sooner the better.

Sitting in the banker's office, my heart sank when I first met Alice. You could tell she was doing her best to stay focused on the questions I was asking however; it was clear her mind was someplace else. Alice's husband had died six months prior to this meeting. Her attention span was limited and you could tell she was not taking proper care of herself. Her face was gaunt due to lack of nutrition and her clothing was unkept. There was no doubt this was a classic case of denial coupled with severe loneliness.

Alice explained she was used to her husband handling all of the finances. Four months had gone by without her making the mortgage payment which was why her home was now in foreclosure, with a sheriff's sale scheduled in three weeks. In true senior form, Alice thought the local bank could help her with this situation but without income and a shaky credit history, the bank was clearly not an option.

It was important for me to try and get as much information from Alice during this first meeting simply because time was of the essence. She did her best to answer all of my questions; however, once she heard the phrase "reverse mortgage" she was not happy. Alice feared that she would not own her home anymore if she went through with this type of mortgage. Educating seniors on the truths of what a reverse mortgage really is, and what it is not, happens to be a big part of my job as a reverse mortgage specialist and CSA (Certified Senior Advisor). I explained that a reverse mortgage would allow her to own her home and that the loan would not have to be repaid until the house was sold; she moved out or passed away.

Her biggest objection in moving forward with a reverse mortgage was that her daughter would not approve of it because that would mean the daughter would not inherit the property <u>free and clear</u> after Alice passed away.

I could not believe my ears! This frail and withdrawn woman who had lost her husband six short months prior and who was three weeks away from losing her home did not want to explore the one option that could actually fix her situation. Her daughter would simply not approve! After taking a deep breath, I suggested sitting down with Alice's daughter to explain. Alice confided in me that her daughter was completely unaware of her financial mess. Alice was too ashamed to admit to her child that she stopped paying attention to the bills. I will never forget Alice asking me "how do you admit to your only child that you are weak and unable to deal with life? A parent is supposed to be the strong one." Wow, this situation was going to be tough! It was at that moment I knew I had to be an advocate for Alice; I had to be strong for her in her time of need. A reverse mortgage was the only way to save her home from foreclosure and if it was something <u>she</u> wanted, I would do everything I could to help her.

After discussing this at length, Alice agreed to a meeting with her daughter and son-in-law. I will share a brutal truth with you: since I made the decision to focus on reverse mortgages, many times I come across situations in which the senior's children <u>want and expect</u> their inheritance. It has been my experience that they have already spent the money (usually due to living above their means and believing their inheritance will eventually bail them out). Unfortunately, this was what Alice was dealing with.

From the first moment Alice's daughter entered the room, she was unhappy, boarding on hostile, and made sure everyone knew. She fired questions at me and I politely answered all of them. Unfortunately, for her, I did not provide the answers she wanted to hear. Alice's daughter was especially upset when I explained that without a reverse mortgage to save the house, Alice would either have to move in with her, live on the street, or come up with a lot of money to cover the past due mortgage payments.

Once I broke it down into these terms - - "the cold harsh truth" - - the daughter "agreed to allow" Alice to move forward with the reverse mortgage.

With everyone finally on the same page, I scrambled to get the HUD counseling arranged, appraisal ordered, and started to pull together the numbers.

As it turns out, the house was worth less and Alice owed more than she originally thought. When it rains it pours because I then found out Alice owed past due utility bills and property taxes. Now it was time to negotiate with creditors! In the end we were able to save Alice's home from foreclosure, pay off all of her past due debts, and give her a bit of money for a savings account.

It has been almost a year since Alice's loan closed. From time to time, I still stop by her house to make sure everything is ok. She's still depressed and very lonely and tells me how much she misses her husband. I listen, offer encouragement, and redirect her attention to the beautiful, positive things in her life.

Often, I find myself thinking about the experience I had with Alice and her selfishly misguided daughter. It would have been so much easier for me to walk away from that headache. In retrospect, I forced the issue because there was no one else to come to her aid. I did not want to see Alice homeless when she had the equity in her home to provide a roof over her head. I am proud to say that I stayed true to my values and was an advocate for Alice.

About Jennifer Hart, Certified Senior Advisor
Reverse Mortgage Specialist

Telephone: 847-210-3280
www.jenniferhartcsa.com

Jennifer Hart, CSA, is caring and understanding of the needs of the senior community. Throughout her years of working with seniors, Jennifer has developed strong relationships with many senior service providers and has developed long term relationships with many of her past clients. Jennifer conducts business using the following as a guideline: to help seniors optimize the equity they have built in their homes thus enabling them to live their retirement years with financial dignity. To have all senior clients experience financial peace of mind and security throughout their retirement years. To increase cash flow and enable her clients to continue to live in the home they have known and loved for years.

Chapter

16

Harry Gordon
Lake Tahoe Mortgage

TAKING CARE OF GRANDMA

(Story told by the Reverse Mortgage Professional)

I have known Carlene Garrison Holland for at least a dozen years. She is a well-known, well-recognized, and well-respected mortgage planner in our region with a passing level of knowledge about reverse mortgages.

Carlene and her uncle were engaged in a discussion regarding what they were going to do about a dwindling line of credit for Carlene's 91 year old grandmother. Several years ago, Frank, Carlene's Uncle secured a line of credit on behalf of his mom which was her primary source of income. His mom suffered from dementia which is why Frank held a power of attorney to handle all of her financial matters. Carlene advised her uncle that it would be difficult, even in the market that existed six months ago, to secure a new line of credit due to Grandma's lack of income and assets.

As it stood, Carlene's uncle was also Grandma's custodian and held her power of attorney; he even began using his own money to subsidize Grandma's basic needs. Her existing line of credit was only going to last a few more months. Frank lived in Friday Harbour Washington; Grandma lived in Santa Cruz, California. He was limited as to how frequently he could see her because of the logistics, and Grandma was totally unable to travel to see him. This situation left Carlene's uncle feeling pressure – pressure because he was her legal custodian and attorney in fact. He also felt pressure because he saw Grandma's funds dwindling, and he felt her finances were his responsibility. He felt pressure to figure out a solution of how to support Grandma during the final stages of her life. Something needed to change – and fast.

Grandma's only asset was her home that happened to be located in Santa Cruz, California, which is a beautiful and desirable ocean front community in Central California. Some family members had made sure their opinions were heard. They said, "Why don't we just sell the house? We'll get a ton of money from the transaction, and we can put mom in an extended care facility." Yet other members of the family were very mindful of their commitment, to keep Grandma in the house, which was her wish.

Carlene saw her uncle struggling with this situation and essentially said, "I don't know much about reverse mortgages, but I know enough to realize that it is our answer to get the money we need to take care of Grandma. I'm going to have Harry Gordon give you a call to discuss reverse mortgages and together, you can decide if this is the best possible solution for Grandma."

I took my time with Carlene's uncle to explain the ins-and-outs of reverse mortgages with him and answer all of his questions. After much discussion, Carlene's uncle made the decision to move forward with the reverse mortgage on Grandma's behalf. However, the process didn't go as smooth as originally anticipated.

Grandma lived in the same lovely home, complete with an ocean view for over sixty-five years. Sixty-five years ago, the property sold for just over $5,000. Today, due to its sought-after location, the property has enjoyed years and years of appreciation and was now valued in excess of $750,000!

This charming home was the one in which she and her late husband raised their children and it held many fond family memories. Before suffering from dementia and fully cognizant, she had made it perfectly clear that she never wanted to move from the house that she loved so dearly. She wanted to be cared for there. This, too, was another challenge that loomed over Carlene's uncle - the need to potentially finance in-home care for Grandma in addition to the care giving that the family members would be able to provide.

Sixty-five years of wear and tear had taken its toll on many of the homes in this waterfront community. There was some termite infestation that needed attention before Grandma's reverse mortgage could close. In response, I had a termite inspection company inspect the property.

Sure enough, termites had infested the home and in the process created one more challenge to overcome. Even so, our goal was to only complete the work necessary to close the loan, which equated to about $30,000. Our objective was not to turn Grandma's house into the Taj Mahal and the pride of the neighborhood; instead, our aim was to make the home presentable and liveable for Grandma.

Carlene's uncle did not have ready access to the $30,000 to pay for the work upfront. I explained the situation to the pest control company, and I asked them if they'd be willing to wait for payment until the reverse mortgage closed. That way, the needed improvements could be made, and Carlene's uncle could pay the repair work from the proceeds of the reverse mortgage.

Thankfully, the termite company agreed to work within our parameters, and Grandma's reverse mortgage closed within 60 days from the time of our first telephone conversation. Carlene's uncle was able to stay afloat until the reverse mortgage closed. We provided a lump sum at closing to handle all the necessary repairs. In addition, Grandma will have a monthly income for the remainder of her life. We were also able to make some long-overdue improvements to the home in order to make it as liveable and functional as possible. The improvements will also help the resale value on the home when the time comes to sell.

Grandma's reverse mortgage also took a lot of pressure off her son. As a matter of fact, during our last conversation, he said, "I think the time may be right for my wife and me to consider a reverse mortgage because we now understand just how well this is working out for my mom."

I think that the greatest sense of accomplishment and joy I received from working on this particular transaction was removing most of the pressure and the stress Carlene's uncle was experiencing from the financial balancing act needed to keeping his mom in her house.

About Harry Gordon

www.reversemortgagecoach.net
775-823-8400, extension 113

Harry, who is a Certified Senior Advisor has been doing reverse mortgages exclusively for four years and has been in the mortgage business for over 14 years. He gained much of his knowledge by teaching continuing education classes for CPAs, Certified Financial Planners and Life Insurance Agents. Mr. Gordon views his profession with extreme pride and seriousness. He is licensed to do business in California and Nevada.

Chapter
17

Brian Cooper
iReverse Home Loans

SILVER LININGS

(Story told by the Reverse Mortgage Professional)

My father taught me many years ago that building relationships is about listening and not talking. I take that life lesson very seriously and practice it each time I interact with a senior homeowner.

Reverse mortgages are my only business. For the past three years I have helped hundreds of seniors nationwide by providing accurate information and recommendations in order to help them make the best financial decisions for their unique situation. I do this by listening to what my clients want to accomplish and educating them about the options available to them.

In order to truly appreciate the story I am about to share with you, you should first know a little something about me; I love what I do. I get tremendous satisfaction in making a difference in people's lives, especially when I am able prove to clients that there are still trustworthy, professional people in the mortgage industry that demonstrate integrity, character and compassion.

I am honest with my clients and explain what I believe to be the best choices for their individual situation regardless of whether or not they decide to apply for a reverse mortgage. In fact, the most important service that I provide to all my clients is a customized "Suitability and Alternatives" report. During our initial conversation, I ask questions designed to help me fully understand their objectives. I then produce a document that outlines my findings and assists me in determining if a reverse mortgage is a suitable product for them. In addition, I list alternative options that may be available, along with the costs, and the pros and cons of each.

Many people have said to me, "What are you doing? Your job is to sell reverse mortgages!" I disagree. My job is to do what I believe is in the best interest of my client. If a reverse mortgage is not their best option, I feel it is still my obligation to give them all of the information they need to make an informed decision. Even if they don't become a client, I have educated another person about the truths of a reverse mortgage and its benefits, and therefore, it was time well spent. So when their best friend or next door neighbor asks them about their experience, they will feel confident passing along my business card, knowing I will be extending the same level of service to each new prospective client.

On a crisp, fall afternoon last year, I received an email alerting me that someone had visited my website and was interested in receiving information about a reverse mortgage. The inquiry was from Kathleen and James - I immediately called to introduce myself as well as answer any initial questions they might have had. During our conversation, Kathleen explained the reason for the inquiry. Their current mortgage had an adjustable rate that was about to drastically increase. If they did not do something soon, their $630 mortgage payment was going to increase to over $1,100 - almost double their current monthly payment! I listened to what they had to say and, together, we decided that a reverse mortgage would be a great option for them to consider.

A couple of days later, I met with Kathleen and James at their home. Their house was beautiful and I could tell they took great pride in it – I noticed they were working on a few home improvement projects in the backyard. We sat down at their kitchen table and began to talk; it was clear to me that both Kathleen and James were a little apprehensive. This was completely understandable to me, as I'd come across this hundreds of times before. After all, inviting a complete stranger into your home to discuss a very personal issue can be a bit unnerving for anyone. James was skeptical, it sounded too good to be true, and in his mind they were too young for something called a "reverse mortgage". Kathleen was just shy of 64 and James had recently turned 66 years old. I assured both of them that they only needed to be 62 years old to be considered for a reverse mortgage and based on their ages, they would most certainly qualify.

James explained how difficult it was to make ends meet in today's very expensive world. He had planned as best he could when he was younger but, with three children and the cost of living increasing at such a rapid rate, finances had become a real challenge. They had refinanced their home a few years prior and now found themselves in a situation where the interest rate on their mortgage was about to adjust. Kathleen and James could not afford a mortgage payment of $1,100 without sacrificing life essentials.

I understood Kathleen and James' situation and could appreciate just how overwhelming this must have been for them. I knew it was important for me to explain the reverse mortgage concept to them in a way that would give them a full understanding of the program. As I outlined the solution to them, I could sense an immediate change in their demeanor and they began to smile again. It was nice to finally see and speak with the "real" Kathleen and James, both full of energy, extremely funny, and such warm people.

I continued to describe how a reverse mortgage would eliminate their mortgage payment, allow them to maintain ownership of their home, and give them the additional money they needed to pay off other debt. They found the answer they had been looking for. At the end of our meeting, I reviewed our next steps and reassured Kathleen and James that I would be by their side every step of the way and available to answer any questions that may arise throughout the process.

Things, however, did not go as simply as we had all anticipated. Not long after our initial meeting, Kathleen called me with some terrible news. James had been involved in a fatal car accident. Apparently, driving home one evening, James was struck by teenagers driving on the wrong side of the road. There were no survivors. Kathleen was suddenly faced with dealing with the loss of her spouse after forty-one years. I felt terrible - such a wonderful man, such a horrible accident, such a tragic loss. The last thing I wanted was for Kathleen to become even more overwhelmed by her financial situation, as now was a time for her to mourn the loss of her spouse, not worry about her next mortgage payment.

But, the fact that she was able to make this telephone call to me at such a difficult time in her life showed me what a strong and courageous woman she truly was. I was honored that she felt comfortable enough with me to make that call so shortly after the accident. Kathleen knew she needed to move forward with the reverse mortgage. She was being a realist. If she and James were financially struggling together, how would she manage on her own? I walked Kathleen, step-by-step through the entire process. The original goals she and James set still had to be met, but due to her recent circumstances, her needs were much greater now.

Over the next few weeks, I spoke with Kathleen on a regular basis, often just to see how she was doing and to offer my encouragement. There were times when I would call and simply listen to her talk - Kathleen just needed someone to lend an ear and I was glad to offer my support in any way I could.

We closed on her reverse mortgage within thirty days. In addition to eliminating her mortgage payment, we were also able to pay county, township, and school taxes. Kathleen would not have financial hardship to deal with anymore.

I am happy to report that Kathleen is doing well and is staying focused on living life one day at a time. She is upbeat and optimistic; still believing the glass is half full, not half empty. She credits her family, including her three children, as well as, the relief she feels from the benefits of the reverse mortgage, in helping her get through her personal tragedy. When I find myself feeling overwhelmed by life's little curves, I am reminded of Kathleen, her strength and her grace which helps to put things back in perspective.

About Brian Cooper

iReverse Home Loans
Telephone: 888-616-2667
BrianReverse@gmail.com
www.reversemortgagetimes.org

Brian Cooper made the decision to specialize in offering reverse mortgage programs because he wanted to make a difference, and sleep well at night knowing that he is helping people nationwide to live a more comfortable life. He takes a sincere interest and listens to what the senior homeowner wants to accomplish. Brian provides accurate information so that people can make the best decisions for themselves. Brian Cooper is a hard working, ethical, honest, caring and respectful person and believes that these traits are what a senior homeowner should be looking for when choosing a reverse mortgage specialist to work with.

Chapter

18

Laura Strickler, CSA
Reverse Mortgage Specialist
Certified Senior Advisor

CLIMATE CONTROL

(Story told by the Reverse Mortgage Professional)

Judy Cleveland was in a very unique situation. There was a very large hole in the roof of her house which would cost approximately $5,000 to repair. There was absolutely no way Judy could come up with that kind of money.

Judy is a resourceful woman and had been working with a local community loan program in Hesperia, California to get funding for the necessary repairs. After spending hours completing paperwork and calling almost weekly to check the status of her pending loan, Judy was assured her loan would be processed. Now she wanted to explore an option to pay off the community loan. This is where Judy met me, Laura Strickler, Reverse Mortgage Specialist and Certified Senior Advisor.

I've been working with seniors exclusively since April of 2001. And while I have helped many seniors through the reverse mortgage process, Judy's predicament sticks out in my mind. I still shake my head when I think about Judy living in a desert community with a huge hole in her roof. Bless her heart; Judy had become a pro at surviving the weather in her desert community. The weather can be frigid at night, with lows in the 30's and then be extremely hot during the day, with temperatures reaching into the 100's.

Initially, I spoke with Judy over the phone. She had already received general information about reverse mortgages, but had questions. Judy was certain that her community loan was going full steam ahead and only wanted the reverse mortgage to pay that off once it had funded. She was very clear that she did not want to move forward with a reverse mortgage until the community loan came through. So, I put Judy on my list to call every few weeks. Can you believe that a few weeks turned into six months?

Each time Judy and I spoke, I learned more and more about her and we began to build a friendship. Judy is a sweet, caring lady and I could not stand by any longer without helping her get funding for the repairs. I made a commitment to Judy that even if she did not choose to work with me to get a reverse mortgage, I promised to assist her in any way that I could.

I started to make regular telephone calls to the community loan processing office and was told that Judy had just missed the cut-off and they were not going to consider any new loans for another six months – until the new fiscal year began.

Judy had already been waiting a few months, and now, six months later, she was still waiting. Judy knew she needed to make a decision about how to get her roof repaired. There was no way she could keep living in a house with a hole in the roof. The seasons were about to change once more and something needed to be done to resolve her home repairs.

Judy felt like she was caught in a tricky situation. She did not want to give one option up for another one that might not come through. I also knew Judy really needed to feel comfortable with whatever decision she made. She was not the kind of person to make quick decisions and relied on her son for his advice. Judy had felt comfortable with her plan of getting the community loan – and then getting a reverse mortgage to pay off that loan. Now, it seemed as though she had no other choice but to figure something else out. Unfortunately, Judy had to deal with the fact that the community loan just was not going to go through.

Finally, after speaking with Judy for over one year, we met. The drive to Judy's house took about 2 hours. Because it gets so hot in the summertime, when I drove up to the house, the entire community looked barren, as if no one lived in any of the homes. Everyone keeps things closed up to save on electricity and keep things cool.

As Judy and I shared a glass of her apricot iced tea and talked about her options, she came to realize that a reverse mortgage was the program to use for funding the roof repairs. I got her set up for counseling and I believe that helped to reinforce the credibility of this (reverse mortgage) program. I made certain Judy understood that if she chose not to move forward with the reverse mortgage, it was ok, that at least all of her options were being explored. Just to be sure all of our bases were covered; we continued to contact the local government offices to lobby for the loan to be closed.

Once Judy went through the required HUD counseling, she made the decision to move forward with the reverse mortgage application. I kept assuring Judy that if the city got the loan done before the reverse mortgage, and if she felt more comfortable going through with that option it would be fine. All I really cared about was making sure she got her roof fixed.

I was very confident that the reverse mortgage would not take long, so I was very pleased that it only took 30 days to fund. She was just 62 when she was approved. Judy was so pleased with her experience, she wrote this heartfelt testimonial on my behalf "Laura made every step of the reverse mortgage process so easy. She explained how a reverse mortgage works, how to qualify for a reverse mortgage and how to apply for a reverse mortgage. Laura is well-versed, trustworthy and cares about her clients."

After Judy's loan closed, her son called me to thank me for helping his mom through the process. He was so grateful that there was somebody there that was reliable and was not taking advantage of his mom since he was not nearby. Calls like that reinforce how I treat my clients. I always think of how I want my parents to be treated and treat my clients the same way. Judy has become a friend rather than a client – I am grateful that I met her and got to know her. I'm glad that she's enjoying her home and not worrying about covering her roof if it rains.

Judy did not need much, did not want much, she just wanted her home repaired. A new roof keeps her cool in the summer and warm in the winter. She is proud of her home, located in a beautiful desert community.

About Laura Strickler, CSA
Reverse Mortgage Specialist

Laura.strickler@cox.net
www.laurastrickler.com
760-518-9839 or 1-800-491-2374

With fifteen years of experience in the mortgage industry, focusing on the senior industry since 2001, Laura Strickler prides herself on upholding her personal philosophy: "If I wouldn't do it for my parents, then I wouldn't do it for my clients." Ms. Strickler takes the time to get to know and (when able to) personally visit each of her clients. Ms. Strickler is on the board of The Angel's Depot (www.theangelsdepot.org), a local non-profit organization providing food to seniors living in poverty.

Chapter
19

Jack Chandler
The Reverse Mortgage Education Center

A LIGHT AT THE END OF THE TUNNEL

(Story told by the Reverse Mortgage Professional)

I have been working with seniors since 1975 and for the past ten years have focused specifically on reverse mortgages. My team and I, at Eagle Nationwide Mortgage Company, a Subsidiary of Eagle National Bank, are not your typical "mortgage folks". We take a unique approach to working with our senior clients.

We do not believe in soliciting business by way of cold calling. Instead, we meet all of our clients through referral sources or direct mail. That means we wait until our clients tell us they are interested in learning more about a reverse mortgage. My team and I do not offer DVD's, Brochures or any other promotional or "sales" items to consumers that request information. Instead, we offer educational publications from independent and reliable sources such as American Association of Retired Persons (AARP), Department of Housing and Urban Development (HUD), Federal Housing Administration (FHA), State Banking/Finance Departments, The Federal Trade Commission (FTC), The American Bar Association (ABA), The American Legion and Fannie Mae, which we personally deliver during a brief ten minute meeting. It is during this initial meeting when I conduct the "fact finder" (which I personally developed many years ago).

This fact finder is one of the main things that set my team and me apart from all of the other reverse mortgage companies out there. It helps me to understand how my clients think about the issues they face such as long-term health care. For example, one of the questions in my fact finder is "What is your plan for long-term care?" Automatically, folks assume I am trying to figure out what kind of insurance plan they have. This is not the case. I am trying to understand what their plan is or determine if they even have a plan. Most families have, at least, a fire escape plan, yet they fail to address life's more likely tragedies and uncertainties.

The answers to these fact finding questions allows me to understand where my clients are going and where they want to go. It uncovers whether they have a mortgage now, their income today, what the income will be should one of them pass away. Admittedly, these are somewhat dark subjects for people to discuss. Most husbands and wives do not want to talk about their mortality. If wives bring this topic up, undoubtedly the conversation becomes tense because the husbands are secretly ashamed of their lack of retirement planning.

It is important to note that during the fact finder meeting, I make it very clear that I am not there to discuss a mortgage. I let them know that I am going to ask a series of general questions. I do not want to know social security numbers, credit card numbers, or account balances. I do not want to know any of that because it is none of my business. But, I do need to know the answers to general questions to help me step into their shoes and point them in the right direction. By using this technique, I can leave them the correct information so they can get educated on the issues unique to their particular situation. Education was exactly what my senior clients; Dwight and Helga were in desperate need of.

It was a sunny day in June when I first met Dwight and Helga. Dwight was retired from the Seattle Times and had held the position of Chief Editor. Dwight had become disabled due to Parkinson's disease, but, just because his body was failing him, did not mean that his mind was. Dwight was still as sharp as a tack; he explained to me how horrid it was to be sitting by, without choices, unable to do anything about his disease or the fate of his wife. If his wishes were to come true, Dwight wanted the love of his life, Helga, to continue to live in their home, to have a team of people to assist her in the upkeep and wanted her to have a new car with a warranty so she could maintain her independence.

Helga sat helpless, watching her partner of 50 years suffer, knowing the end would not be pleasant. Both Helga and Dwight thought that she would never be able to afford to continue to live in their home if Dwight passed away due to this terrible disease. Their 2,000 square foot home had a huge backyard and the cost to maintain that large of a home seemed out of reach for Helga. She thought that she was doomed to a life in a condominium after his death. Along with a limited retirement fund, their paid-in-full home was all that they had. Unfortunately, Dwight and Helga were outliving their retirement nest egg.

After completing the fact finding process, at the end of that first meeting I left a variety of materials for them to review and educate themselves with, all regarding reverse mortgages. I left them books from Fannie Mae and AARP as well as articles from the Washington Department of Financial Institutions, the American Legion, and the FTC.

It was during the second meeting with Dwight and Helga where I learned that they had chosen to leave "everything" (their finances) the way they were and Helga would just have to downsize and live on a shoestring budget. At this point, it was my job to bring my clients back to reality. I reminded Dwight that it was not fair to Helga to be left to make financial decisions while mourning the death of her husband. How could they predict how Helga would react after she lost her life's partner? It makes more sense to make difficult decisions, like this, when you have your partner around as a sounding board to discuss your questions and concerns. I left that meeting with hopes that my feedback would at least get them to openly discuss their situation.

Approximately one week later, I received a telephone call from Dwight requesting that I come back to his home. He had taken the past couple of days to reflect on a reverse mortgage and realized it would be the light at the end of their tunnel. Instead of looking towards the total darkness and sadness of Helga being forced to make difficult financial and housing decisions at the most inconvenient time in her life, he realized a reverse mortgage would allow Helga the option to retain their home instead of losing it. Six weeks later, Dwight and Helga's reverse mortgage was complete.

The first thing they experienced together as a couple was to shop for a new car for Helga. Dwight had such a great time watching Helga choose the color of her new car. The second thing they wanted to tackle was the landscaping. Because Dwight was wheelchair bound, Helga wanted him to be able to enjoy the outdoors in the privacy of his own home. They were able to afford high-quality landscapers to care for her yard and upgraded the landscape by having trails and sprinklers added along with additional plants, trees and bushes, all indigenous to the state of Washington.

Before Dwight passed away, his disease got worse and he also developed cancer. Under their previous circumstances, if Helga and Dwight did not get involved with a reverse mortgage, she would have been forced to put Dwight into a nursing home. Because of the reverse mortgage funds, she could afford to hire almost round the clock help (costing approximately $5,000 per month) and replace the carpet with hardwood floors to help move Dwight more easily throughout the house while he was still alive.

Helga could pay for home health care so Dwight could live out the remainder of his life in the comfort of their home. A reverse mortgage was indeed the light at the end of a very dark tunnel.

About Jack Chandler

The Reverse Mortgage Education Center
www.HECM.net
1-800-540-6033

Since 1975, Jack Chandler has been working with seniors in the areas of Medicare health plans, long-term care planning, life insurance and, for the past ten years, reverse mortgages. Mr. Chandler's vast experience allows him to evaluate his client's needs and explain in simple terms how to best utilize the resources available to mature Americans. Mr. Chandler prides himself on taking the time to listen and relate to all of his clients and treats each as though they were his own parents.

****

In March of 2008, Mr. Chandler was diagnosed with Kidney Cancer which quickly spread throughout his bones before treatment could be given.

Through this tough time, his clients have brought such sunshine to Jack's life; letters, notes and cards consistently pouring in.

Not only has Jack dedicated his life to helping others, but even as he boldly faces death he has found the strength, everyday, to continue to take a personal interest in the well being of his clients, discussing their needs with his best friend and business partner, Travis De Renzo.

Not one person, who has really gotten to know Jack, can honestly say that he hasn't left an imprint on their hearts and lives. I know he has truly touched ours.

Chapter

20

Sylvia Williams
Robert Williams
Sequoia Reverse Mortgage

FINDING THE RIGHT SOLUTION

(Story told by the Reverse Mortgage Professional)

My husband Robert and I (Sylvia) are business partners and make a fantastic team because our strengths are so different yet complimentary. Prior to working in the reverse mortgage industry, Robert was a field service engineer, specializing in electronic control systems. He is extremely analytical and always wants to get as many details as possible from our clients. He believes that this wonderful financial program (reverse mortgage) literally changes lives and he is on a mission to help as many seniors as he can. In my former life, I taught elementary school and was a college professor. I truly believe that education is the key to helping people with the reverse mortgage process and my ability to help borrowers understand these types of mortgages has been instrumental to our success. Together, we meet with clients and review all of the financial information in order to make the best recommendations for our clients.

We pride ourselves on making absolutely certain that our senior clients understand everything and to some degree, we become their advocate. We educate our seniors about the reverse mortgage industry and then we show them options because if a reverse mortgage is not right for them we are the first ones to tell them! In our senior client, Mr. Fulcher's case, a reverse mortgage was the perfect solution although; it took a little bit of research to come to that conclusion.

You see, Mr. Fulcher was in a very unique situation. His story is not one of financial trouble; instead his story is of heartache. The reason Mr. Fulcher wanted to meet with us was to discuss the option of a reverse mortgage to financially assist his daughter and three teenage grandsons. Sadly, his daughter was diagnosed with terminal cancer and has less than eighteen months left to live. With her illness, she is unable to work and is struggling to make her $1,200 monthly mortgage payment and quite frankly can barely feed her growing teenage sons. Since his daughter insisted on living independently, Mr. Fulcher wanted to do whatever he could to provide the best care for her and her boys and make their lives as comfortable as possible during the last months of her life.

The love Mr. Fulcher has for his family is striking and quite impressive. My husband vividly remembers during the initial meeting, that Mr. Fulcher talked about his daughter's situation, becoming emotional. Everything in his life revolved around the family. He wanted to do anything he possibly could for them which is how he made the decision to pursue a reverse mortgage.

Mr. Fulcher knew that he was living in an asset, his beautifully paid off home! Everything in his home was immaculate and well decorated, including wicker fencing all the way around the property. The home is handicap friendly for Mr. Fulcher has health issues to the point that he has two motorized wheelchairs and a walker at each entrance inside his address. Thankfully, all of his medical expenses are completely taken care of due to the fact he served in the United States Army. Mr. Fulcher was savvy in his retirement planning. His home is paid in full, no medical expenses, and has a proven portfolio.

Mr. Fulcher shared his plan to help his daughter with Robert during their initial meeting. Mr. Fulcher's intent was to take his reverse mortgage money in one lump sum, which he estimated would equate to approximately $140,000 and then pay off as much of his daughter's mortgage as possible. Robert listened to Mr. Fulcher's plan and understood that Mr. Fulcher was serious about making sure his family was financially cared for. Time was of the essence and Mr. Fulcher was serious about doing whatever it took to help his family.

Later that afternoon, as Robert and I reviewed Mr. Fulcher's information I was very concerned by the idea of him using one lump sum from a reverse mortgage to pay off his daughter's mortgage. At the end of the day, his daughter was still going to have those monthly payments that she could not afford and he would have nothing left to live out the rest of his life.

We really wanted to make sure that he was not making a decision based on emotions. Our goal was to determine if a reverse mortgage would benefit him, if not, we would find other ways to help his daughter.

So we called Mr. Fulcher in order to express our concerns. His bottom line was that he needed to help his daughter as quickly as possible with the mortgage payment. His idea of using the money from a reverse mortgage was the only one he had. I suggested that we at least evaluate a few other options before making a decision. The first thing I wanted to do was to review his daughter's monthly mortgage statement. Mr. Fulcher faxed it over to us and after review; I got his permission to call his daughter. We analyzed her options regarding what she could do with this mortgage. Go to her lender get the rate adjusted, etcetera, etcetera, etcetera.

We determined that a reverse mortgage was a good option; however it was not appropriate for Mr. Fulcher to use his lump sum to pay down his daughter's loan. Instead, we recommended using that money to assist with the monthly payments and he would of course have money left over. Once his daughter passes away, he would then have the choice to either continue paying for and buy that home or just use it as a rental property.

Mr. Fulcher was extremely pleased with our recommendation and shared with us what he was going to do with the rest of the money from his reverse mortgage. Mr. Fulcher has two other children and wanted to be fair to each of them. So, he helped to finance his second daughter's new massage therapy business and helped his son purchase a mobile home. In addition to making the monthly mortgage payments for his ill daughter, he sent her and her boys to Hawaii and to Disney so they can make as many memories as they can while she is still living. Mr. Fulcher even treated himself to a new truck to haul his scooter and kitchen cabinets refurnished!

Robert and I were happy to be able to help Mr. Fulcher find the right solution that would best meet his needs.

About Team Williams

Robert Williams
Direct: (916) 716-1413
Toll free: (888) 424-2688

Sylvia Williams
Direct: (916) 719-4683
Toll free: (866) 523-1959
Website: www.reversemortgagetrainingsolutions.com
Email: sylviawilliams@comcast.net
My Blog: http://activerain.com/blogs/coachinginreverse

Robert & Sylvia Williams live in Elk Grove with their two cats. Both have been in the reverse mortgage industry for nearly four years and have originated approximately 700 loans between them. Both Robert and Sylvia are licensed Real Estate agents. Sylvia has earned her Certified Senior Advisor (CSA) designation. They are both committed to getting the word out about this wonderful program so that seniors can live their later years with peace and happiness, free from financial worries.

Sylvia is so committed to the correct training of reverse mortgage consultants that she developed a training course for loan professionals and is a partner in Reverse Mortgage Training Solutions.

Chapter

21

Robert Griffin
Griffin Financial Mortgage, LLC

LIVING IN MY RETIREMENT PLAN

(Story told by the Senior Client)

One day while sitting on my front porch trying to get a bit of fresh air, I noticed a contractor's work truck in my neighbor's driveway. It was clear to me that they were in the process of having their home remodeled. I wondered how they were able to pay for something like that. Without home owners insurance, I was at a loss as to where I was going to come up with money to repair my smoky, water-logged home. A week before, my home had almost burned to the ground. A fire had started in the kitchen and spread to the living room. The fire department did a great job to contain the fire so it did not damage the rest of the house too much. Thankfully, I was able to get my son out of the house safely. That boy means the world to me, and I do not know what I would do if something happened to him.

What a terrible predicament this was to be in. I needed to figure out what I could do. It was clear what I could not do which was bring my handicap son back into this mess of a house. It was bad enough I was still living in these conditions. Times were tough before the fire, and now they seemed almost too much to bear. As it was, we did not have heat or hot water in our home. We just could not afford to pay the electricity bill. My family had lived in this home for almost 50 years, and it never seemed as though we had enough money for repairs. The good times got us through the bad, but there was never enough for extras. I am not sure if words can express just how frustrated I was. I kept thinking, "I am 80 years old for crying out loud. How much more do I have to endure? When are things going to get easier for me?"

I went to the local bank and looked into getting a home improvement loan, but it was not an option with my fixed income. I could not even afford homeowners insurance; I could not make the monthly payments on a home improvement loan.

Believe it or not, I am actually a roofer by trade. Of course, I am retired, but that is how I used to make my living. I decided to swallow my pride and take a walk over and have a chat with my neighbors. Maybe they knew something I didn't about how to pay for home repairs.

The contractor was a nice man and seemed like he knew what he was doing. He told me my neighbors were paying him with money from their reverse mortgage and informed me that Robert Griffin helped them get one. To be honest, I was not sure what a reverse mortgage was, but I was determined to find out. I used the neighbor's telephone to contact Robert Griffin, and when I got him on the line, he seemed like a nice man and politely answered my questions. Robert wanted to come to the house and talk to me face-to-face, which I agreed would be a good idea.

I could tell Robert was a bit surprised about the conditions I was living in, and I couldn't blame him. I was surprised too. We sat outside on the porch to talk simply because the inside of the house was a complete disaster. After an in-depth conversation, Robert thought a reverse mortgage might just be possible. The big question would be the cost of the repairs that would be needed in order to pass FHA inspection.

We decided to get an initial bid from the contractor that the neighbors used to make sure it was going to work. The contractor determined I needed a new roof, a whole new kitchen (including new wiring), and a fire alarm just to get my home up to the building code standard and pass inspection. The contractor also recommended a new heater, air conditioner, new flooring, and new ceilings if there was enough money. I added new appliances to my wish list. All in all, the bid came in around $30,000. According to Robert, based on the value of my home, my age, and the amount of equity I have accrued over the years, a reverse mortgage would easily cover the cost of everything on my wish list. I had to pinch myself when Robert shared the news with me. To this day, I still shake my head in disbelief that all these years I was living in my retirement plan and never realized it.

We had to have the contractor do the work in advance before Robert could submit my reverse mortgage application for approval. Can you believe that my reverse mortgage not only covered the costs of everything on my wish list, it covered the cost of all of the past due taxes I owed as well as new bath fixtures, cabinets, and a few new pieces of furniture?

My son was able to move back into our home once the work was complete. I am ecstatic now that everything has been refurbished, and it seems like we live in a brand new home. I am so happy that I have actually told a few of my younger children who are now in their 60's that they should call Robert at Griffin Financial Mortgage. I know they could benefit from a reverse mortgage like I did. Robert went the extra mile for me to make sure I was taken care of. He also made sure that I had basic necessities like heat and hot water that my son and I lived without for so many years. For that I will be forever grateful.

About Robert Griffin

Griffin Financial Mortgage, LLC
888-415-1955
Robert@griffinloans.com
www.griffinloans.com

A twelve veteran of the mortgage industry, Robert Griffin specializes in reverse mortgages and has earned the accolade of number one reverse broker in the southwest for three years in a row. The owner of Griffin Financial Mortgage, LLC, based in Fort Worth, Texas, his memberships include the National Association of Mortgage Brokers (NAMB), the Mortgage Bakers Association (MBA), the National Reverse Mortgage Lenders Association (NMRLA), and the Better Business Bureau (BBB).

Chapter
22

Monte Rose

A VOICE YOU'LL REMEMBER

(Story told by the Reverse Mortgage Professional)

Jimmy Weldon is a TV and Hollywood icon. He began his show business career by creating and hosting the first children's TV show in Dallas, Texas. His sidekick Webster Webfoot accompanied Jimmy across America for the next 19 years. He provided the voice for the little orphaned duck in the Yogi Bear cartoon series. You may remember his signature line. When the little duck would be asked, "Where's your momma?"…the little duck would sadly reply, "I ain't got no momma." Jimmy is an author and motivator. He flys himself to personal appearances and speaking engagements in his Beechcraft Bonanza.

He answers the telephone before the conclusion of the first ring and says, "Hi, this is Jimmy, sorry to keep you waiting." Jimmy is the personification of "inspirational living." He is a man who gives new meaning to the term positive aging. And, by the way, he's 85 years young. Visit his website, www.jimmyweldon.com, for all the details.

Jimmy has the "secret sauce" for life, so I asked him, "What's the source of your zest for life?" He gave me a two-part answer.

"First, I commit to accomplishing something everyday - no matter great or small. When my head hits the pillow, I want to feel a sense of accomplishment. Whether it's as small a task as doing the dishes or as great as inspiring a group of salespersons or seniors, I made a contribution."

"Second, I stay connected with people. People are what life is about. I refuse to be lonely. If I can't get out, I call them on the phone. Before I call it 'a day', I reach out and 'touch' someone."

When I first spoke to Jimmy, he'd sold his precious Bonanza airplane. A dip in the stock market had taken its toll on Jimmy's finances, and he was no longer able support his flying avocation.

Knowing how much he missed the joy of flying, a neighbor suggested Jimmy investigate the use of a reverse mortgage to buy another airplane. First, He called his niece to discuss this option with her. The conversation yielded a very important question, "Would the lender 'take the house'?" Jimmy's next call was to a friend, a retired banking executive, who also had some serious reservations about the program. "Was it safe?" "Will you receive exactly what you're promised?"

Three days later, Jimmy received a telephone call from his banker friend who said, "Mr. Weldon, I've been out of the banking business too long. The reverse mortgage concept is a fantastic equity releasing tool. Go get your money to buy an airplane."

However, there was a problem. Jimmy didn't want another airplane, he wanted <u>his</u> airplane back, and finding it would be like searching for a needle in a haystack.

He began to surf the Internet, and actually found it. His next step was to research reverse mortgage companies. Financial Freedom's website caught his eye, and that's how I met Mr. Energy, Jimmy Weldon.

During our initial conversation, Jimmy and I spoke at length about using a reverse mortgage as a tool to buy his airplane back. Jimmy's home was paid off, and he had enough money for his basic living expenses. His chief concern was getting his airplane back. He decided to move forward with the reverse. So, he completed the paperwork, and received his counseling, and we began to process his application.

Then, out of the blue, he landed a contract with Yahoo! for two commercials. This turn of events certainly changed Jimmy's financial picture. Perhaps he didn't need a reverse mortgage.

According to the AARP Public Policy report, (a National Survey of Reverse Mortgage Shoppers, published in December 2007), most people utilize a reverse mortgage to alleviate financial pain. Some persons explore the reverse mortgage for a strategic purpose, but don't follow through with it. Jimmy was one who made a strategic decision.

One of the reverse mortgage benefit options is the growing Line of Credit, and Jimmy decided to allow his home to create a contingency fund that compounded over time. Although he didn't need it today, he might need it in the future. The cost of "set up" was small in light of the appreciation of his home over the next few years. He was now creating a nest-egg that would grow tax-free, until he needed it.

For five years, Jimmy did not touch his reverse mortgage Line of Credit. He just relaxed, knowing that the reverse mortgage was his safety net. Jimmy's borrowing power increased by almost 50% during the "waiting period." And it became a wonderful source of "peace of mind."

About a year ago, Jimmy made the decision to tap into his line of credit. With the support of his family, he began a systematic monthly withdrawal. "My nieces and nephews told me, it was my money, and I should spend it."

Imagine his surprise, when he reviewed his monthly reverse mortgage statement and found that his available benefit was not decreasing by the amount of his withdrawal. The positive compounding feature was replenishing his Line of Credit. This was truly a Win/Win for Jimmy. The waiting period had actually increased his benefit substantially, and his prudent withdrawal schedule would enable him to be "worry free."

Today, Jimmy doesn't think twice about how much it costs to put fuel in his airplane. He continues to travel and speak spreading positive and uplifting messages. And Jimmy does his best to tell everyone he knows about the benefits of a reverse mortgage.

About Monte Rose

Telephone: 1-800-516-0545
www.monterose.com

Monte Rose has helped hundreds of seniors obtain a reverse mortgage during the past 17 years. His career path has taken him from salesperson to manager to executive to consultant. He is an accomplished speaker and widely quoted industry expert. The Monte Rose business menu includes consulting, sales training, productivity tools, and speaking.

Chapter

23

Shannon Daniele
Quest Funding Inc.

MISCONCEPTIONS LEAD TO TWO FORECLOSURES

(Story told by the Reverse Mortgage Professional)

Years before I started Quest Funding Inc., I owned a company called Rescue Funding which was designed to assist people whose homes were in foreclosure. We did this by offering hard money loans, which means we gave them a loan based on the equity in their home. That is how I first met my senior client, Mrs. Snicker.

Mrs. Snicker's home was in foreclosure, and it was just three days before the trustee sale when I first spoke to her. In retrospect, she lost her house because of owing only $30,000. Thankfully, we were able to help by lending her the money to save the house as well as pay for $20,000 worth of renovations. These improvements made the home handicap-friendly for her ailing husband so he wouldn't have to live in a convalescent home.

Unfortunately two months later, I received a telephone call from the investor who financed Mrs. Snicker's loan making me aware he and his partners were going to foreclose on Mrs. Snicker's loan due to non-payment.

I knew something must have been terribly wrong so I contacted Mrs. Snicker. During our telephone conversation, I learned that Mrs. Snicker was not accustomed to paying bills or managing any personal finances. Those responsibilities had always been her husband's before he fell ill. She confided that she was absolutely clueless about how to handle the situation and was too embarrassed to talk to anyone else about it. I assured Mrs. Snicker that I wanted to not only help (once again) save her home from foreclosure but also to help her put some systems in place so she would never find her home in a foreclosure situation again.

A few days later, I met Mrs. Snicker at her house to investigate what was going on. Sitting in her kitchen over a cup of coffee, we first reviewed all expenses for the Snicker family. As I went through the stack of bills, I was genuinely surprised by what their monthly expenses were. Mrs. Snicker and her husband had a car payment, insurance, not to mention maintenance of the house, food, and medical bills. Due to her husband's illness, they incurred a lot of expensive co-pays and of course, gasoline to and from doctor appointments. It became clear to me that Mrs. Snicker was taking care of what was most important to her, her husband. Paying the mortgage just wasn't a priority.

As we reviewed their income, much to our surprise, there was money available that Mrs. Snicker just wasn't aware of. As it turns out, her husband had a sizeable pension, but the only thing Mrs. Snicker saw on a regular basis was their social security checks. With only the social security check to support them, there wasn't enough money left over after paying the regular monthly bills. No wonder the mortgage wasn't getting paid! Now that we'd developed a plan to pay their monthly expenses, we needed to find a way to pay back their past-due loan.

I left that meeting with a renewed sense of appreciation for the Snickers situation and was determined to save Mrs. Snicker's home (for a second time) from foreclosure. I spent the next few days talking to lenders and researching the best possible options for Mrs. Snicker. I reviewed her situation over and over in my mind, and this is what I came up with: Initially, we took a client who had lost her home to foreclosure and gave her a loan. We took this approach because of the misconceptions associated with reverse mortgages. Just like many seniors, we bought into the untruths about reverse mortgages. After we gave her the loan, she went in foreclosure again.

I really believed that there should be some responsibility on the part of the lender so this woman (and anyone else getting a hard money loan) doesn't go back into foreclosure. That is when I decided to explore other ways of lending which lead me to learn about reverse mortgages. I wondered if reverse mortgages weren't so bad after all. I learned as much as I could about the ins and outs of reverse mortgages and came to the realization that reverse mortgages are powerful and positive when used properly. In this case, a reverse mortgage would not only save Mrs. Snicker's home from foreclosure, but it would also allow her to spend time completely focused on her husband and remove her financial worries.

I contacted Mrs. Snicker to share the good news with her. I told her that a reverse mortgage would be the vehicle used to save her home. She was relieved and extremely grateful. I gave Mrs. Snicker the next steps needed, and she promised to take immediate action.

At this point, Mrs. Snicker's husband was extremely ill. She didn't want to give him any news - good or bad– and he didn't want to spend their precious time together sorting out finances. She arranged for power of attorney so she could make decisions without bothering her husband.

After all of the paperwork was in order and the reverse mortgage was finalized, Mrs. Snicker was ecstatic. The reverse mortgage provided some of the best gifts she had ever received. It provided her with quality time to spend with her husband who would be able to live out his last days in peace.

Today, Mrs. Snicker is an advocate for reverse mortgages and is an unofficial spokeswoman for Quest Funding, Inc. She speaks to local community groups (such as Rotary) on a regular basis and tells her story on how a reverse mortgage saved her home and changed her life. Additionally, she talks to everyone she meets about reverse mortgages, shares her personal experience, and outlines the benefits.

If they want to learn more, she will schedule an appointment for someone from my team to meet. This is her way of saying thank you for everything we did for her.

Mrs. Snicker is the reason I was introduced to reverse mortgages and for that I am grateful. Today, I am so passionate about presenting this option for my clients, especially for senior homeowners in default or foreclosure. It's important to me to dispel the myths about reverse mortgages. I want to be sure people have the right information and not fall into the trap I fell into years ago. I am so passionate about educating people about reverse mortgages that I conduct two seminars each month. I also lend my expertise to community leaders, church groups and senior citizen organizations, and I highlight how a reverse mortgage can positively impact the life of a senior.

About Shannon Daniele

Quest Funding, Inc.

562-256-5779

Mr. Shannon Daniele, age 38, is the co-founder and executive vice president of Quest Funding, Inc. and Quest Mortgage Fund, LLC, which holds a 100 million dollar security permit. He has been a certified CMIA real estate broker since 2005. Mr. Daniele is a tireless advocate of financial empowerment for senior citizens and takes pride in serving his community. He has been praised by Realty Times as "the best resource for senior citizens who want reverse mortgages."

Chapter

24

Dennis Smith
Mortgage.Shop LLC

IN DIRE STRAITS

(Story told by the Reverse Mortgage Professional)

My senior homeowner client, Mrs. Guire, was referred to me by the Phoebus Improvement League which is a non-profit group that aids the revitalization efforts in the local community.

The Phoebus National Historical District is an 86 acre section of Phoebus that is made up of the historical business area as well as a considerable number of homes. Of the 426 buildings included in the district, 60 percent are now eligible for a combination of federal and state tax credits of up to 45 percent for qualified preservation or rehabilitation.

As it turns out, Mrs. Guire's home was located within the Phoebus National Historical District but was unfortunately in jeopardy of being condemned by the city due to much needed and significant repairs. The good news was that her home qualified for preservation which is how the Phoebus Improvement League got involved.

To bring Mrs. Guire's property up to city code (and out of the brink of condemnation), major repair work was needed. A new roof, an upgrade of the electrical system, new windows, and removal of dead trees was estimated at $45,000. Mrs. Guire could not even tap into her homeowners insurance for assistance because she had dropped her coverage when she could no longer afford it.

The result of all these circumstances left Mrs. Guire nearly homeless, without the means to pay for the repairs needed to meet city code, and she was unable to qualify for a *regular* loan. Having been retired for a little over 15 years, Mrs. Guire sadly lived hand-to-mouth. She was a widow and her children could not afford to help pay for the repairs. To put it mildly, this was an extremely difficult situation.

When I first met with Mrs. Guire, she wasn't exactly thrilled by the idea of a reverse mortgage. Without an income, she was unable to get a traditional mortgage which left a reverse mortgage as her only option. Unfortunately, she believed all the common misconceptions that are out there about reverse mortgages. She was worried that she would lose her home to the city and then to a lender if she moved forward with any kind of mortgage. Needless to say, I had my work cut out for me to help Mrs. Guire keep her home.

Our first meeting took place in my office as Mrs. Guire insisted on coming to me. To this day, I still believe the only reason she came into my office was to make sure I owned a legitimate business! I was surprised when she strolled up to the door. She didn't have a car and walked into town each week to go to the bank and the post office, fill her prescriptions and take care of other errands. Since my office was in town, she merely added visiting my office to her list of weekly errands.

We pride ourselves on being honest and always doing what is in the best interest of *our* clients, even if it means recommending that they use an option other than a reverse mortgage. In this case, I knew that a reverse mortgage was the only way to save Mrs. Guire's home, and made educating Mrs. Guire about what a reverse mortgage really was (and what it was not) my first task. The moment she understood the FHA reverse mortgage program was not only going to help her save her house, but that it was also going to allow her to retain ownership of her home was music to her ears and a huge sigh of relief for her. Additionally, she was comforted in knowing that when she passes, the house can still go to her heirs.

Now that I had her permission to proceed, it was time to roll up my sleeves and get busy choosing contractors. The Phoebus city code office recommended a few contractors for her consideration, and I *and the Improvement League* helped her check them for proper licenses and reviewed their record with the Better Business Bureau (BBB). Because of her particular financial circumstances, *we* also worked with Mrs. Guire to negotiate payment terms with the contactors. We had to get the contractors to agree to do all the repair work before receiving any payment so the loan could close.

Thankfully, it wasn't that difficult to identify a good team of contractors who were willing to forego compensation until the work was finished and the reverse mortgage process was complete. Once I shared Mrs. Guire's story with them, they were more than happy to help any possible way they could.

With the construction underway, it was time to get Mrs. Guire's insurances in order. She was in need of homeowners and flood insurance. *My office associate, Allison Trevathan* befriended Mrs. Guire and volunteered to take Mrs. Guire to the local insurance company. To this day, Allison and Mrs. Guire get along famously, and they have built a solid friendship.

The next step was to identify any programs Mrs. Guire could take advantage of to aid her as she moved forward. She qualified for the city real estate tax relief program, and we made sure measures were taken so she was properly enrolled in this program. Also throughout the construction process, *we* made it a point to stop by her home to see the progress for myself and make sure everything was on track. Mrs. Guire's situation had become a personal matter to me and our entire office, so it was important for me to stay on top of this project to ensure everything was completed correctly and on-schedule.

Once the repairs were completed, we were able to close on the reverse mortgage loan. Mrs. Guire's home was finally fully repaired and met city code! After paying every contractor in full, she still had the money for living expenses and her homeowners insurance and flood insurance premiums. She will never find herself in the situation of having a nearly-condemned home that she can't afford again.

Even though Mrs. Guire was originally a skeptic about mortgages in general, she now refers new clients to us all of the time. She stops by the office every three to four months for a visit and has become a part of our office family. And every time she stops by the office, she tells me how well she can now sleep at night knowing her home is repaired and her financial needs are no longer an issue. And each time she tells me, it is still so nice to hear!

About Dennis Smith, Mortgage.Shop LLC

www.ReverseMortgage.Pro
757-722-6800

Dennis Smith has been in the mortgage, insurance, and investment business for over 25 years. He has written several financial articles for news publications, been a regular guest on television and the past *16* years has hosted the "Family Financial Expert Hour" on multiple radio stations. Dennis also earned the Virginia Mortgage Brokers Association's Award of Excellence in the Field of Reverse Mortgages *and his company has been named WAVY TV 10's Mortgage Expert On Your Side along with WVEC TV 13's Mortgage Specialist.* Listen to Dennis host "Debt Free Express" on Norfolk's WTAR 850am atwww.wtar.com.

Chapter

25

Kimberly Douglass
Dunne & Company Reverse Mortgage Specialists

RETAINING MEMORIES

(Story told by the Reverse Mortgage Professional)

My purpose for specializing in the reverse mortgage industry is to help seniors. My philosophy is to do my absolute best to help as many seniors as I possibly can. Less than one year ago, I started working as a reverse mortgage professional and I am so glad I did because it gives me the opportunity to meet and help seniors like Ms. Conway.

Ms. Conway's home is distinctive because it is in a building called the Bay Shore Royal. It was originally a posh hotel. It is located close to MacDill Air Force Base and served as barracks in World War II. Now it is a condominium. This building, now Ms. Conway's home, holds very special memories for her. When the building was a hotel, it was one of the top places to go in the Tampa Bay area and was known for the dinner and dancing offered on the tenth floor. It also happened to be where she had her first date with her husband.

Ms. Conway discovered her amazing condo thanks to her daughter who called her one day and said, "Mama, I found the perfect home for you."

Ms. Conway responded, "Okay. Well, tell me where it is?"

"No, Mama. I'm going to bring you there!" And she brought her mother to this condo in the Bay Shore Royal. Ms. Conway cried because it triggered so many special memories - up on the on the tenth floor dining and dancing with her late husband.

At 79 years old, the rising costs of living expenses combined with a negative adjustable mortgage on her Bay Shore Royal condo was just too much for her to financially handle. Ms. Conway was searching for help because her current mortgage interest rate was about to adjust again and get much higher.

I met Ms. Conway after she received a direct mail piece from us and called our office for information. Initially, she and I had a brief telephone conversation where she shared with me that she'd actually been told by another company that she could not have a reverse mortgage. The closest I could figure their reasoning for this was that her condo was not on the pre-approved FHA list. With just a little extra effort and time, I was able to have her condo approved.

As I previously mentioned, the historical building Ms. Conway lives in has a lot of sentimental value, and her main objective was to be able to stay in her home. She had already downsized when she moved from her home to a condo. She and her late husband collected antiques, and when she moved to the Bay Shore Royal, she had to part with many household items and collectibles. She simply could not imagine having to give up any more.

Furthermore, she did not want to be faced with moving at age 79. Besides, she is exactly where she wants to be. She enjoys an amazing view of the water and lives near her two children and five grandchildren who she visits with regularly.

Initially, both Ms. Conway and her children were skeptical of the idea of a reverse mortgage since she had been previously told this would not be possible. The children advised her not to get her hopes up, at least not until she was approved. Once Ms. Conway was approved, her children were completely assured of this option. I found it wonderful that Ms. Conway's children were so supportive and involved. They wanted to make sure their mother stayed in the condo that meant so much to her. They knew there had to be a way to avoid her mortgage payment going from $630 to $780 per month. Most people do not think $150 is a big difference in a monthly payment; however, when living on a fixed income, $150 represents basic necessities such as food and medicine. It also limits the ability to take your grandchildren out for ice cream!

Even though the process took three and a half short weeks, Ms. Conway would call me to ask, "Are you sure this is going to happen?" That is one aspect of my job that I am not sure I will ever get used to - the fact that nobody believes the process will come through for them. Instead, everybody believes that it is too good to be true. I am here to tell all seniors that a reverse mortgage is not too good to be true. It is a wonderful and viable option for many seniors!

Since Ms. Conway's loan closed, we have kept in touch. We enjoy going to lunch at the current top restaurants in town. As a matter of fact, I talk to her almost every week. We go over any mail that comes in that she is not sure about. For example, some companies send seniors confusing and misleading marketing pieces that imply that they may need additional insurance or that they must refinance, which is simply not true. These weekly chats allow me to help Ms. Conway make sure she isn't being taken advantage of, and I am happy to help.

Ms. Conway's reverse mortgage not only allowed her to stay in her memory filled condo, but it also allowed her to receive a sizeable check that she can use to pay off debt and put away for a rainy day. But of course, the biggest benefit for Ms. Conway is not having a mortgage payment of $780 hanging over her each month.

I'm so happy I met Ms. Conway and am even happier I could help her! I really like helping my seniors and hearing their life stories. Most of all, I enjoy bringing them the good news and seeing stress replaced with joy.

About Kimberly Douglass

Dunne & Company Reverse Mortgage Specialists
1.866-627-0711 toll free
KimberlyDouglass@ReverseMortgageSpecialist.Info
www.ReverseMortgageSpecialist.Info

Kimberly Douglass lives in Valrico, Florida with her son, Austin. She is a mortgage originator specializing in reverse mortgages and mortgage modifications. Kimberly is affiliated with Dunne & Company Mortgage Lenders where she heads the department of reverse mortgages and she heads the department of mortgage modifications. Kimberly is also a consultant to Tampa Bay area financial advisors.

Chapter

26

David Olson
AI Mortgage.net

A STARLET'S STORY

(Story told by the Reverse Mortgage Professional)

My senior client, Melody Prudent is one talented lady. Years ago, she made a living by singing, dancing, playing the piano, and even starred in a variety of operettas. The baby grand in her sitting room reminds her of those days in the spotlight.

When I first met Melody, she was 78 years old and running out of money. Unfortunately she had never applied for social security because she simply did not think she needed it. Ten years earlier, her husband had passed away and left her with quite a bit of money in savings and investments; however, now the money was dwindling.

But Melody did not reveal this important detail during our initial meeting. In fact, she acted like she was just exploring the idea of a reverse mortgage. She did not express much enthusiasm towards our meeting or the idea itself. See, six months before meeting with me, she'd met with another mortgage agent regarding a reverse mortgage. And even though she'd completed the required counseling, she did not get the impression that this agent was sincere and as a result, hadn't made any decisions.

Throughout our initial meeting, I did my best to answer her questions and explain how a reverse mortgage works. However, when I asked her questions about her situation, Melody was vague in her answers. She made it clear that before she could make any decisions, she needed to talk to her financial advisor who oversaw about $10,000 of her investments. I understood her need to discuss this with her financial advisor, and I assured her that my intentions were to help her any way that I could. Our meeting ended with me promising to give her time to think through her option and telling her I'd contact her again in a few weeks.

True to my word, over the next year, I continued to call Melody. During each telephone conversation, she acted like she was still considering a reverse mortgage but was clearly not ready to meet with me to discuss the next steps. Out of the blue, she called me one day because unbeknownst to me, her needs started to become greater. Melody requested to meet with me and stressed, "the sooner the better."

During this second meeting, I finally discovered the reason for Melody's mysterious attitude. She had no income and like many seniors, she did not know how to handle her situation. Melody had some money left over from her investments but was not much, which was why it finally became urgent to get her reverse mortgage done. She confided in me that when she called her financial advisor he advised her to do a forward mortgage. She was running out of money, and he was talking to her about a forward mortgage! Was he crazy? Thankfully, Melody knew better than to get herself further in debt with a "regular" mortgage. Melody admitted she was ashamed that she spent the money her husband left her and felt somewhat taken advantage of by a few home repair companies.

It really was a shame that she had these unfavorable experiences, first with the reverse mortgage person she'd met with and then with her financial advisor. No wonder why each time I spoke to Melody, she was hesitant to make any decisions! To make matters worse, her health was deteriorating. She had cataracts and had to hold documents no more than six inches away from her face to read them. Also, Melody had very few teeth left as they were knocked out in a fall, and she did not have any money to replace them. Her driver's license was expired because of her poor eye sight. She had no homeowners insurance, no social security, and was unable to get around because she was too proud to ask for help. As if all those things were not bad enough, because she never applied for social security, her medical expenses were not covered by Medicare. Melody needed help and fast!

With a clearer picture of Melody's financial situation, I recommended she seriously consider a reverse mortgage. That said, I made it clear that I wanted her to feel comfortable with not only her decision but also in working with me. Melody told me how much she appreciated my persistency over the past year and felt I never tried to push her into making any decisions. Actually until this point, I had never even made the recommendation for her to consider a reverse mortgage because I did not have enough information. That was enough for Melody to put her trust in me.

When Melody finally made the decision to move forward with a reverse mortgage, believe it or not, that is when the real challenges began. Unfortunately, Melody did not have any documents that reflected her social security number on it and did not have valid photo identification. We needed proof of her social security number in order to complete the reverse mortgage application.

So, I drove her to the social security office and when we finally got to the window, we discovered she could not apply for social security without a picture ID. Although she had driver's license, they would not accept it because it was expired. Then, we took a trip to the Department of Motor Vehicles and sat in another endless line. Thankfully, Melody was able to get a photo ID. Our next step was to get a new HUD counseling certificate because the original one Melody did with the previous reverse mortgage broker had expired.

After almost a year, we were able to finalize Melody's reverse mortgage. What a blessing a reverse mortgage has been for this starlet! Melody was able to take enough money to get both her cataracts and teeth fixed. She now has access to $755 per month which she does not even come close to spending. Additionally, she has a $50,000 line of credit for future expenses.

Melody still has a few more hurdles to overcome as she still does not receive social security benefits. What we finally learned was that Melody Prudent has been her stage name since the age of 16. When she went to apply for social security benefits it was found that was not her legal name, and although she has used that name for more than 60 years, it had never been legalized in court. So, now Melody is in the process of getting a court order to legalize her name as Melody Prudent so that she can proceed with social security and medicare.

I still see Melody from time to time, inviting her to lunch to get her out of the house. My hope is that now that her eyesight and teeth are fixed, she'll meet new people and feel more comfortable being social. Eventually I hope Melody will share the rest of her starlet story with me, too.

About David Olson

Affordable Interest Mortgage
303-570-1148

I have been in the Financial Services Industries for over twenty-five years and the Reverse Mortgage business for more than four years. With uncompromising standards of Integrity, Honesty, and Service; I give my clients the confidence of knowing that their transactions will be completed professionally and ethically. Making a difference in someone's life, how do you describe that feeling? I am passionate about working in the Senior market. I put away my selling shoes and put on my educator shoes realizing also that we are not in the instant gratification business. There are families, trusted advisors, etc to be consulted. When you close a Reverse Mortgage, you'll know why you're in the business. You won't need anybody to say anything. You'll see it in their faces. d.olson@aimortgage.net

Chapter

27

Sue Haviland
Reverse Mortgage Success

FIRST-TIME HOMEBUYER

(Story told by the Reverse Mortgage Professional)

One of the best kept secrets in the entire reverse mortgage world is that a senior citizen can actually purchase a home as long as it is going to be their primary residence. My senior client, Clara, officially became a first-time homeowner at the age of 82 years old.

This is how I helped make Clara's dream of owning her own home a reality.

I met Clara through her daughter-in-law, Laura, a real estate agent. It might seem a bit unusual, but I market reverse mortgages to real estate professionals in addition to seniors. In the course of speaking with real estate agents one-on-one, I ask them to think about how a reverse mortgage might fit into their overall business plan. In one of my conversations with Laura, she mentioned that her mother-in-law was 82 years old and was unhappy with her living situation. Clara lived in an apartment for years, and Laura told me how she would have loved to see her mother-in-law have her own home.

When I proposed the idea of Clara using a reverse mortgage to purchase her first home, Laura was stunned. No one had ever shared this information with her before, and she was certainly interested in learning more. After taking a few minutes to explain the process so she had a clear understanding of how it worked, Laura suggested we meet with her mother-in-law. We could explain this home buying opportunity through a reverse mortgage and see if it was something that she wanted to explore further. I knew I could count on Laura to keep Clara's best interests in mind, as I would as well.

Clara is one spunky 82 year old lady. To say she was skeptical at first would be an understatement. I was fully aware that without her daughter-in-law's support, Clara would never have believed there was a way for her to purchase her own home at 82 years of age and never make a mortgage payment. To her, it seemed too good to be true, an opinion expressed by many seniors.

Clara was not shy about sharing her unhappiness with her living arrangements. She did not like renting and never quite found a rental property that felt like home. Clara told me that she would lay in bed and dream of what it would be like to own a home. She would think about paint colors, furniture placement, and even inviting friends over to visit. Clara wanted to live in a home that she was proud of.

Those reasons were enough to get Clara excited to learn more about how a reverse mortgage might be the way to make her life-long dream a reality.

Clara had something working in her favor. The good part about her renting for all of those years was that she did not pay a lot in rent, and over the years, she'd saved a substantial amount of money. This meant she had money available for a down payment.

We started by determining the price range Clara was going to be able to afford by using a combination of cash available as well as the reverse mortgage proceeds. We spent some time playing with the numbers and made sure it was something that Clara was comfortable with. When it was all figured out, I assured her that the numbers would work and that she could move into a property and never make a mortgage payment.

With Clara, the education process was a bit more involved because she had never owned a home. She was truly a first-time home-buyer at age 82. I had to educate her on the entire buying process as well as the reverse mortgage process. By the end of that first meeting, Clara understood the concept and was confident that she really could become a home owner. Clara gave notice at her apartment that she would not renew her lease, and Laura helped her start the process of searching for a property.

It did not take long for Clara to find exactly what she was looking for. The property she felt most comfortable with was a condominium. She knew that at her age, she wanted a low maintenance property and did not need a large place. Fortunately, she found several to pick from that she could comfortably afford. She would easily be able to pay the condo fees and the property taxes using her regular monthly income.

At 82 years of age, Clara was able to give up apartment living, which she truly did not like. We were able to put her in a property of her own with no mortgage payment which completely turned her life around. She is so happy and it has made such a difference in her quality of life.

On the day of settlement, as they were preparing the settlement sheet, it was questioned as to why Clara was receiving a first-time homebuyer discount. We had to explain that she truly was entitled to this discount off of her closing costs. Everybody got a kick out of meeting Clara, an 82 year old first-time home buyer.

I suspect that if I'd had a conversation with Clara prior to this happening and asked her if she thought she would ever become a homeowner, she would have said no. She would not have believed that there was a way to make home ownership a reality. Now four years later, Clara has actually mentioned to her daughter-in-law, Laura, that she would consider selling her condo and buying another condo with another reverse mortgage to be a bit closer to her daughters.

This was a first not only for Clara but for me as well. While Clara became a first time homebuyer at age 82 because of a reverse mortgage, this was the first time I had ever used a reverse mortgage to help someone purchase a home. I guess it is safe to say that we are both big fans of the capabilities found in a reverse mortgages.

About Sue Haviland

Reverse Mortgage Success
www.asksuehaviland.com
www.reversemortgagesuccess.com
443-667-0389 or 410-557-0294

Sue Haviland is a reverse mortgage consultant in Baltimore, Maryland, and the founder of Reverse Mortgage Success, a leader in training and educating loan originators about reverse mortgages.

Haviland has worked in the lending industry since 1981 and has been originating reverse mortgages for the last six years. She has helped hundreds of families across the country in the last several years by sharing her knowledge of this market in articles and presentations before various professional organizations as well as the public.

Chapter

28

David VerMeulen
VanDyk Mortgage Corporation

EASING FINANCIAL PAIN

(Story told by the Reverse Mortgage Professional)

At 64 years old, my senior client, Lillie, was in financial pain. Eight years before I met her, she'd left her corporate career behind to pursue a dream of owning an in-home daycare center. Lillie loved children and was tired of commuting into the city everyday for a 9-to-5 job that did not fulfill or challenge her. Lillie quickly realized that owning a business, even out of her home, was expensive. Obviously, she could not rely on a weekly paycheck to pay her bills. Plus being a new business owner did not pay as much as her corporate job. Clients come and go in the first few years of business which makes it difficult to forecast income. Further, Lillie had refinanced her home in order to make improvements for her in-home child care business and to pay the bills while establishing her business. Lillie was barely making ends meet each month and some months, she was in the red. She needed money to help cover her personal and business expenses so she was not stressed out each month about how her bills were going to be paid.

Lillie received a direct mail piece from my office offering reverse mortgage products as a financial tool for seniors. She began researching this option and after everything she read thought it might be a good decision for her. Lillie called me to see if a reverse mortgage would help relieve her financial stress. During that initial conversation, she told me she owed $100,000 on her house and wanted it paid off. According to her calculations, eliminating her monthly mortgage payment would help tremendously.

We made the decision to meet in her home the following week. I always use a two-step process when working with seniors: education first, and then if they decide to go forward, I schedule a second visit to complete the application. Our first meeting went smoothly. We discussed her situation, and I explained exactly how a reverse mortgage works. Lillie already had a solid understanding of reverse mortgages, so the information I provided filled in any blanks she had. It made sense to her, and she decided at that first meeting that a reverse mortgage was the right solution for her situation.

Once the application was complete, we moved the process forward by ordering a title search and having the appraisal done. When we did the title search, we uncovered that Lillie owed a little bit more than $100,000. In fact, she owed $212,000.00 on the first mortgage, and approximately $30,000 on a second mortgage. Needless to say, those numbers threw a major wrench in the plan. I called and said, "Lillie, you owe far more than you originally told me, and I can't help you."

She got very emotional on the phone and started to cry. It was then she explained to me that the first mortgage holder was threatening foreclosure, and she'd taken out a second mortgage to help her son with some bills that he had, and because of that, her son was now also listed on the title of the house.

Although late, I now had her entire financial story. In retrospect, I think the reason she did not share this critical information sooner was that she was embarrassed and overwhelmed. I assured Lillie that no matter what her financial situation was, I would do my best to help her any way that I could. We decided to meet a few days later.

Before our next meeting, I discussed Lillie's situation with John Donovan my Reverse Mortgage business partner, who is also an attorney. John and I came up with some ideas as to how to help Lillie. Our plan was to have Lillie and her son give me signed permission to talk to the first and the second mortgage holders to see what we could work out. They agreed, and I immediately went to work. I explained to the mortgage lender what we were trying to accomplish by using a reverse mortgage proceeds, which are based on the appraised value of the home. I wanted to convey to them that if they put Lillie's house in foreclosure, they would do two things. For one, Lillie would be left with nothing, and due to a short sale, the second mortgage holder would be left "holding the bag." Secondly, they would inadvertently kill the values of the homes in Lillie's neighborhood. One foreclosure in the neighborhood can cost every homeowner $50,000, to $100,000 in appraised value, which can make a significant difference to anyone in that neighborhood trying to refinance or take out a Reverse Mortgage. The impact would be felt not only by the homeowners but by the bank as well.

Ultimately, the first mortgage holder consented to take a short refinancing of approximately eighty cents on the dollar. They also agreed to give the second mortgage holder $2500 of the Reverse Mortgage proceeds. The second mortgage holder agreed to take the $2,500 from the Reverse Mortgage along with a small additional amount from the homeowner in exchange for subordinating their mortgage to the reverse mortgage.

Just when I thought we were on our way to helping Lillie achieve a reverse mortgage – one that would save her $1500 a month in cash flow, put her in a better financial situation, eliminate the tremendous financial stress and save her home from foreclosure, we discovered one more hurdle to overcome. As we finalized the negotiation with both mortgage holders, the Commonwealth of Massachusetts put a lien on the house. Lillie's son had an unpaid state income tax bill.

This was definitely an emotional rollercoaster for Lillie who, upon receiving this news, was fully prepared to move out of her home. She knew we were going to try to negotiate with the Commonwealth but was not sure it would work.

The good news was once I got permission to talk to the Commonwealth and explained what we were trying to accomplish with the Reverse Mortgage and we were able to work out an agreement that was satisfactory to all parties. The bad news was we did not have a lot of time to get the Commonwealth to modify their lien and pave the way for the Reverse Mortgage. Lillie was on the verge of foreclosure, and if we did not meet our commitments to the two mortgage holders, the sheriff was going to show up at her front door and she would be removed from her home.

By the grace of God, the timing worked out, and we were able to save Lillie's home from foreclosure. She continues to run her childcare business and loves it more each day. Her reverse mortgage was able to pay off the first mortgage and pay down part of the second mortgage which left her with a manageable monthly payment. Each time I speak with Lillie, she makes it a point to thank me for changing her life for the better.

About David VerMeulen

VanDyk Mortgage Corporation
617-901-8902
800-605-1153
dvermeulen415@vandykmortgage.com

David VerMeulen has over 30 years of experience in financial services, including corporate retirement plans, annuities and individual retirement income planning, design and sales. Dave's professional life began with owning and operating a retirement plan TPA. After building the organization it was sold to Dun and Bradstreet.

Most recently Dave completed his corporate career at Fidelity Investments in Boston as part of the retirement income planning team that built the new web based retirement income planning tool.

Dave's Reverse Mortgage business is based in the Boston area and serves senior homeowners throughout Massachusetts and the surrounding states.

Chapter

29

David E. Gardner
Advent Financial, Inc.

A PROMISE KEPT

(Story told by the Reverse Mortgage Professional)

It is not often that I have the chance to work with two adult siblings who cared so completely for their aging parents and shared the same vision of what they wanted for their final years. It was clear from the start when Carol and Bonnie first contacted me that they had their parent's best interests at heart. They were searching for a financial solution to the challenge of providing a way for their parents to stay in their home together. Their mother now needed daily home care due to chronic illness. At the same time, their dad was in the early stages of dementia and could no longer be responsible for his wife's care. The thought of their parents, now age 86 and 87, living out their remaining years in a nursing home or apart from each other was simply not an option.

Carol and Bonnie were already helping their parents manage affairs and were painfully aware that savings that once seemed sufficient would not sustain them much longer. Both parents had decent retirement incomes, but this alone was not going to be enough to pay for 24/7 care. Even though both daughters lived nearby and were already taking turns caring for their parents, they recognized they could not keep this up indefinitely. So the daughters needed a solution: How would they pay for their mother's needed care and still keep their parents together in their home? What made it even more difficult was Carol and Bonnie had promised their mom they would do whatever it took to keep them both comfortable in their own home, no matter what.

With their savings dwindling, the only remaining asset their parents had was the home. Fortunately, like many senior homeowners they had substantial equity in their home. In fact, they had no mortgage or home loan of any kind to pay off. As many adult children do, Carol and Bonnie thought first about a home equity loan and how that could be used to pay for their mom's home health care. It did not matter to Carol or Bonnie that using home equity would impact their inheritance. They even thought about taking home equity loans on their own homes.

The other issue the sisters needed to consider was the fact they both had well-paying jobs with good benefits. They each needed those incomes for their own families and to continue to build equity in their own retirement plans. If either or both had to quit working now to care for their parents, they would walk away from jobs during their peak earning years, with negative impact on their own retirement nest-eggs and social security benefits over many years into the future. One way or another, there was going to be a cost involved even if they could quit their jobs to care for their parents themselves.

When their parent's health started to decline, they spent a lot of time planning along with help from the family's elder law attorney. This ensured both daughters were on the same page in terms of what they were and were not willing to do with their parents care. Carol had durable power of attorney for legal affairs and Bonnie had medical power of attorney for health and medical decisions. Because they had already worked through these issues, they were in a much better position to consider financial alternatives. Sometimes the hardest part, where pressing health care needs are involved, is getting everyone in agreement and working toward a solution. Then again, not all siblings are like Carol and Bonnie, who were of such like mind when it came to their parents, you would've thought they were twins!

As far as financial alternatives were concerned, they quickly determined that home equity loans were at best a temporary solution, not to mention you have to make monthly payments on them. Carol and Bonnie then remembered hearing about reverse mortgages from television commercials and other advertisements. Then when they received a letter about its availability from their local bank, they became intrigued. They felt comfortable when they realized there was someone local they could talk to instead of an unknown person on the other end of an 800 phone number to some unknown part of the country.

The daughters called up their local bank and spoke to the person who had helped them with their forward mortgages and whom they had known for years. The bank let them know they had a program to help them. This gave them confidence to look further into them so the next thing they did was go back to their attorney and run the idea by him. The attorney understood their situation and encouraged them to pursue it, but with the suggestion they be sure to deal with a reputable lender who was experienced in working with seniors. Carol and Bonnie agreed it was time to learn more about how a reverse mortgage might be a solution for their parents' financial needs.

I first met Carol and Bonnie at the bank and spent a lot of time answering their questions and learning more about the objectives they were trying to meet.

As they explored the pros and cons of a reverse mortgage for their parents, they ultimately decided it would be best for us to meet with their parents. Despite them having power of attorney, it was important for the daughters to get their parents involved in the process. Although their mother was not physically healthy, mentally, she was still as sharp as a tack. As for their father, he said that as long as "the boss" (the boss being his wife) was happy, he would be happy.

During our second meeting at their parent's home, Carol and Bonnie helped set the stage about how a reverse mortgage could help them and said how I was working together with the bank to offer the program. They said "Mom, we've looked at this and Mr. Gardner is going to explain everything to you." The daughters made sure all of their mom's questions were answered and acted very much as if they were independent advisors for their parents. Their mother kept asking the daughters, "Well, how do you feel about it? Do you think I should do this?" They would respond, "What is important is what you want, not what we want. We just wanted to make sure that you had somebody like Mr. Gardner to talk to so that you got the right information. The decision is yours." The daughters really tried to be neutral about the decision at hand. To be honest, I had never seen adult children remain neutral in quite this way before.

Ultimately, their mother gave the green light to proceed, and based on my previous conversations with Carol and Bonnie, I was able to provide them with an analysis using my careful estimate of their home's value. I consider this estimate to be very important to define a client's expectations on what to expect in funds. I would not want to over-estimate this to Carol and Bonnie just to get their business. Since I knew going into the meeting our goal was monthly income, not debt retirement, we would be able to release a significant amount of funds to meet their needs. The assignment I had given the daughters was to identify the exact amount needed each month for their parent's care. Inclusive of their current retirement income, they needed an extra $4,500 each month.

Because they owned a nice home in good shape in an area with strong values, we were able to generate a substantial amount of funds. Fortunately, they owned it free and clear and it turned out to be worth nearly $30,000 more than the daughters expected. It was now clear that Carol and Bonnie would find the solution they needed for their parents with a reverse mortgage.

Once the home appraisal was completed, we then re-ran our calculations and ended up with just over $227,000 to work with, after all financed closing costs were deducted. From this, I showed them how they could receive the needed $4,500 per month as a Term Advance which would guarantee this payment to them every month for 48 months. For their convenience we arranged for this to be deposited directly into their parent's bank account. At my suggestion, they also received 8,000 in cash for immediate expenses and used the remaining balance of $26,000 to set up a Credit Line to serve as their emergency fund for unexpected expenses or to let grow and use later to extend the monthly income they are receiving.

Even with a paid home care service providing for the bulk of their parent's needs, Carol and Bonnie still take turns making daily visits to check in on their parents, help with household chores, get groceries in the house and to get them to doctor's appointments. After all, no plan can possibly pay for everything or eliminate a family's participation. And even if it could, as Bonnie and Carol have since told me, it could not substitute for the time they now get to enjoy being with their mom and dad.

A reverse mortgage is a powerful tool. It is more than just numbers or analysis of benefits vs. closing costs. In working with Carol and Bonnie I realized I had helped preserve four lifestyles. I preserved her mom and dad's lifestyle by keeping them together in their home. And, Carol's and Bonnie's lifestyles were also preserved. They can work full time and contribute to their own retirement funds while still spending enjoyable time with their parents. But that was not all.

Not long ago, I gave Bonnie and Carol a call to see how things were going. Was the reverse mortgage doing everything for them they had hoped for?

There was a pause on the other end of the phone and then Bonnie's voice broke just a bit as she began to speak. "Mr. Gardner," she finally said, "yes, everything worked out just as you said and it really has been a blessing." Then she said, "I guess you hadn't heard.....our mom died last month." Before I could barely express my regret, Bonnie said, "You know, the best thing of all was that we kept our promise to our mom. You can't imagine how much that meant to her and to us."

Carol and Bonnie had always thought that mom would outlive dad, who continues to live in his home and is assured of many more months of care thanks to his thoughtful and loving daughters.

About David E. Gardner

Advent Financial, Inc.
dave@adventmoney.com
www.adventmoney.com

Dave Gardner lives in Crofton, MD and specializes in senior financial issues. He is a mortgage originator and producer-manager
affiliated with Advent Financial, Inc. in Bel Air, Maryland. He has
nearly 30 years experience in financial services, including an extensive background in life and health insurance. Dave has consulted
with area banks on the reverse mortgage program and has taught
continuing education classes to other professionals on senior topics,
including retirement planning, long-term care and reverse mortgages. He can be reached at (301) 221-9931 or call Advent Financial, Inc.
at (410) 803-8900.

Chapter

30

Mark Yesh
Colonial Mortgage Corporation

FINALLY WORRY-FREE

(Story told by the Senior Client)

I want everyone reading this story to know how a reverse mortgage from Mark Yesh helped my husband and I achieve personal and financial independence.

Our financial downturn started when my husband lost his pension when the cigar company he worked for from 1945 to 1977 closed their doors.

We were always under the impression that if you work hard and contributed to the company retirement plan, you would have enough money to live off of during your retirement years. My husband and I never knew that losing his pension was even a possibility. We had sub-standard savings from some real estate investment properties. It wasn't much, and we could never have lived on that money. Thankfully, we have two sons who helped us through some very difficult times. Both of our sons went without so we could have a few extra dollars each month for the basics such as food and gasoline. Can you imagine being in a situation where you have to rely on money from your children to make ends meet? That was difficult for us as we do not want to be a burden to them. We felt like we are the parents who should take care of them.

Being over 50 years old and searching for a new job was a real challenge for my husband. As it turns out, he could never find work that paid as well as his job as a cigar salesman. With no alternatives, we sold our home and downsized with hopes that the move would positively affect our lives.

Not long after our move, I faced some major health issues after a terrible car accident. My back was broken in several places; my left arm was fractured, and I spent 19 days in the hospital. Unfortunately, my health got worse as the doctors discovered multiple blood clots throughout my body which, of course, resulted in even more medical bills. Our health insurance was unbelievably high. We were paying almost $800 per month for the two of us.

We sold our home yet again, downsized, and moved into a condo. Despite our best efforts to live a meager lifestyle, the cost of living and our taxes kept increasing. My husband and I got to the point that no matter which way we turned, we couldn't make ends meet.

We heard about a reverse mortgage, and because our condo was paid in full, we thought it might be the answer to our financial situation. My husband and I asked our sons to take the lead in researching the pros and cons of a reverse mortgage. They discovered that a reverse mortgage might be a good option for us; however, when our first point-of-contact (the loan officer at our son's bank) couldn't help us, they referred us to Mark Yesh at Colonial Mortgage Corporation.

Mark came to our home to meet with my husband and me as well as our sons. During our meeting, we discussed the possibilities of a reverse mortgage, and Mark was extremely helpful in explaining the process to us. Mark took the time to ask us a lot of questions and wanted to make sure we evaluated all possible alternatives. We shared with Mark that we desperately needed financial help.

While a reverse mortgage sounded good, my husband and I did have our doubts. We were of the mind set that we wanted to leave the home to our kids. Ironically, our sons were the ones that encouraged us towards a reverse mortgage because they had their own homes and families. They didn't need our home when we were gone. Our sons made it clear to us that they could take the money they were giving us each month and start using it with their own families. A reverse mortgage would be a win-win for everybody.

Mark gave us a few weeks to think about what we wanted to do. Ultimately, my husband and I made the decision to move forward with a reverse mortgage, and Mark visited us at our condo once again and set up the required counseling. Mark took care of everything for us. Our reverse mortgage went through without a hitch!

We were amazed at the immediate relief experienced. There was money in savings account for the first time in years, and we even now have a nice amount in our checking account. Thanks to Mark Yesh, we are worry free for the first time in years.

It gives us pride to know our sons are worry free and know we can buy what we need. Our car broke down about two months ago and because of our reverse mortgage, we could buy a new car for the first time in 20 years! It is a beautiful car, and we happily paid for it in cash!

Thanks to our reverse mortgage, we are relieved! Thank you Mark Yesh for all your professional care.

About Mark Yesh, VP of Reverse Mortgage

Colonial Mortgage Corporation
Livonia, Michigan
1-800-260-5484
myesh@colonial-mortgage-corp.com
yeshucan@yahoo.com

Mark has over eleven years of experience in the mortgage industry, and since April of 2004, he has dedicated his time solely to reverse mortgages. He has trained and developed a team of Reverse Mortgage Specialists who consistently help over 250 seniors each year. Mark continues to originate reverse mortgage loans for seniors in the Detroit-metro area. In addition to training Reverse Mortgage specialists, Mark has given dozens of seminars on the topic of Reverse Mortgages. He believes in "helping senior homeowners enjoy life!"

Chapter

31

Amy Catling, CSA
GIA Mortgage Corporation

INSURANCE FOR SOARING GAS PRICES

(Story told by the Senior Client)

To be honest, I did not really need a reverse mortgage. I was more or less just looking into it to see how it might help my wife and me. At my age - I'm 77 years old - I don't know how much time I have left on this earth and wanted to be prepare for any unforeseen situations. I had a few bills that would be nice to pay off and with the increasing price of gas; I really needed a new car. Even though I have been retired for years, I work with our local community action program and help transport seniors to the doctor and right now, it is costing me money! If gas prices kept increasing, it was going to be important for me to have an automobile that would be more gas efficient.

Like everyone else, I saw quite a few commercials on the television about reverse mortgages. I was skeptical about talking to a stranger; therefore, I made the decision to attend a seminar hosted by a local mortgage company. The evening did not turn out as I thought it would. The presentation was rushed and they did not leave enough time at the end for anyone to talk to them. Instead, they wanted me to schedule an appointment with them. Why in the world would I want to waste more time with people who made me feel like I was unimportant?

But the one good thing coming out of that presentation was I now had enough information to pique my interest, and I was not going to give up on researching the reverse mortgage option. I read an article in the newspaper and decided to call the toll-free number at the bottom in hopes of speaking directly with the author, Amy Catling from GIA Mortgage Corporation. As luck would have it, I was able to speak directly with her and I will tell you that talking to her on the phone was altogether different than talking to the people from the other company. I felt comfortable with Amy and talking to her reminded me of talking to my sister.

A few weeks later, Amy met my wife and me at our home. We really hit it off! We sat there and we joked and laughed and so forth. We sat for a few hours and went through everything including the home equity loan that we were using to fill up the oil tank and for some things around the house.

When Amy explained that a reverse mortgage would replace the home equity loan, it made a lot of sense to us. We would get rid of the monthly payment, freeing up income every month that we could use for something else and still have extra money for emergencies. Amy knew we were not ready to make any decisions that day. It was nice not to feel any pressure from her. She left me with the biggest stack of papers - over 90 pages of information to review.

Can you believe that I read every single last word on every one of those 96 pages? I had a lot of information to digest and wanted to take some time think about this decision. I continued my research on the Internet and would write down my questions then call Amy and ask her different things. She was so helpful. All I would have to ask is, "Will you come back?" and she was here in no time.

My wife and I took some time and discussed this decision with our son. He felt that we should get the money for our house and enjoy our lives. It was important to him that we did not worry about leaving the house to him or any other equity, for that matter. My son even said that it really was not any of his business. He stressed that it was our decision to make.

Within a month after our reverse mortgage closed, we bought a new blue Toyota Prius with some of the money. As it turned out, I took out almost $5,000 more than I needed. I did not want to have it accessible because I did not want to spend it! Amy helped me figure out how to complete the paperwork for sending the money back, and how to access it should I ever want more money.

For now, we chose the option of sending in monthly payments, so we can pay down our loan. What is nice about it is we do not have to make a payment, yet there's no penalty for paying down the loan when we have extra money. It was important for us to be smart about this money so we could keep it for a long time and be able to use it as a financial tool.

The reverse mortgage has given us added financial security - knowing that it's going to be there. One of the best things about the reverse mortgage is that I don't have to worry about losing my home - as long as I keep my homeowners' insurance and taxes current. Let gas prices go through the roof! I'll still be here!

Since meeting Amy and getting our reverse mortgage, my wife and I sleep much better at night and are much happier today than we ever were. We are free and clear of all of our debt which is just unbelievable!

About GIA Mortgage Corporation

Telephone: 207-251-0633
Amy Catling, Certified Senior Advisor

Amy strongly believes in customer service and sincerity. She is a graduate of Assumption College with a degree in Biology with a concentration in Biotechnology. After entering the workplace in 1994 she soon realized her passion for working directly with people and using her creativity to solve problems. She became a technical sales representative for a Massachusetts Biotech company and worked in the sales and marketing department until the birth of her oldest child. This is when she decided to make Maine, where she had summered for years, her permanent home.

After staying at home with her four children, she decided to enter the family business. Amy's goal as an originator is to make every transaction simple and successful. In order to do this, she strives to understand her customers' wants and needs; this in turn lets her find the best solution for each individual situation. www.seacoastreversemortgage.com

GIA Mortgage is licensed in ME, NH, MA, and CT.

Chapter

32

John Barlow
Cornerstone Home Mortgage

PRESERVING A HOME
FOR THE THIRD GENERATION

(Story told by the Senior Client)

The home I live in was originally purchased by my father back in 1957 for a little under $30,000. Today, that same property is worth $1.8 Million. Not a bad investment, huh? I cared for my parents in this home before they passed away. It holds so many fond memories for me and my three sons. The problem was I was struggling to afford the upkeep of the home when the tax bill was over $1,000 a month.

My father was just a normal guy - an engineer by trade. Back in the 1950's, there were a lot of people who would sell off properties to put their kids through school. When people were selling, my dad was buying. He was such a smart man. Our family home is located on a beautiful spot on prestigious Mercer Island, and today, you can see the Seattle Seahawks headquarters from my back porch. Mercer Island has the second highest property values in the Seattle area. And it just so happens that my neighbors are millionaires and even a few are billionaires. I guess you could say that I am a millionaire based on the value of my inherited property. But let me be clear - I might be a millionaire on paper because of this property, but that is it.

I am just a working class woman that happens to live surrounded by rich people. It has become increasingly difficult for me to make the normal tax and insurance payments, which continue to increase, let alone any of my regular living expenses. At age 66, I rely on Social Security for my income. I was at a point of such frustration, and I needed some direction and guidance. Keeping this property in my family was extremely important to me, and I needed to figure out how I could accomplish this goal.

I made arrangements to meet with my financial planners to review my options. Unfortunately, I quickly learned I would not qualify for a conventional loan because I did not have enough income each month to repay the loan. My financial planners thought a reverse mortgage might be a solution for me but was not completely sure so they called one of their trusted partners, John Barlow from Cornerstone Home Mortgage, to see if he could help me.

We connected with John via conference call and through all of the questions we fired at him, he kept his professional demeanor. My financial planners wanted to know the state of the current mortgage market and what my options were. I liked John's approach and felt comfortable with the ideas he suggested. By the end of that conversation, we determined a reverse mortgage would be the best solution for me to pursue. I was hopeful this would help ease my financial burdens and allow me to stop worrying about how I was going to pay my bills each month. To be honest, I was not looking for a lot. I was just looking for enough to make my life a bit easier.

I invited John to my home to review the terms of a reverse mortgage, and one of my sons joined us for this meeting. I wanted to make sure I was not missing anything. After all, this property would someday be passed onto my sons. We wanted to be sure that we'd stay in control of the property if I decided to do a reverse mortgage. My son had questions about the fees, the structure, how long it would take to get the money, and how long the payment was going to last. It was a good thing my son was there since I rely on him to help me with financial decisions.

After answering all of our questions, John made it a point to design something that would give me the right amount of money per month and give me a small line of credit for emergencies. I could tell John really had my best interest at heart and worked hard to make sure he structured a program for me that exceeded my expectations. My son and I were comfortable and decided to schedule the required counseling and appraisal.

Before John left, we showed him around the property. During a recent storm there was a large tree that came down and hit the boathouse behind our house. That repair project had been postponed because there just was not enough money to cover the costs. I asked

John if there would be enough money to repair the boathouse, and he promised to see what he could do.

John Barlow came through for me and my family with flying colors. A few months later, my reverse mortgage was finalized. I can not tell you how relieved I feel now that I know this property will stay in our family. I can also tell you that I am thrilled not to have to pinch pennies each month for groceries and medicine. Living that way was not fun at all! My sons are also happy to know that I do not have to bear the financial burden of making those hefty monthly tax and insurance payments.

A reverse mortgage changed my life for the better. It has given me the freedom to live without financial headaches. I am sure my parents are looking down from heaven and smiling at me, knowing their hard work was preserved.

About John Barlow

Cornerstone Home Mortgage
www.reverseinfo.net
888-289-1512

John Barlow owns Cornerstone Home Mortgage with his brother Tim Barlow. Cornerstone is a full service mortgage brokerage servicing all types of mortgages for the residential market. We are licensed in the state of Washington and have been originating mortgages since 2001. Cornerstone currently has over a quarter billion in loans under management.

Chapter
33

Tom Ritter
Axia Senior Lending Solutions
A division of Axia Financial, LLC

UNDERLYING ISSUES

(Story told by the Mortgage Professional)

Sandy and I were introduced to one another by clients of mine. They were a couple that had already explored a reverse mortgage with one of my competitors and yet they did not understand how the program applied to their needs. They needed guidance. When I met with them, we spent an hour and a half together, talking about their goals, objectives, needs and desires. In the end, they were able to identify the reverse mortgage as a solution. They elected to go forward with me to secure a reverse mortgage.

After every first meeting, I always give my client a pad of paper and ask two questions: (1) "Will you promise to write down all of your questions? Because I promise to answer them." And (2) "Do you know anyone that would benefit by this product and if so, will you introduce me?"

Within two days of our initial meeting, the couple introduced me to Sandy. As soon as they understood the solutions a reverse mortgage offered them, they could clearly see how it could also help their friend.

That week I called and introduced myself to Sandy; she was expecting my call. The first question I asked was, "What are your goals and objectives?" She explained that she wanted to complete some work around the house - a new roof, some new windows, and paint the interior and exterior of the home. It was important to her to have extra money to travel to Ireland and New York to visit her children and grandchildren. I spoke with Sandy over the phone several times before our first face-to-face meeting.

When we finally met, it was as if we had been friends for some time. Over a cup of coffee, we talked about her children and grand-children as well as her late husband. When we finally got back to business, I asked her the same question, worded in a different way, "Sandy, what do you want a reverse mortgage to do for you?" Her answer was consistent with every other time I asked the question, so I understood that we were heading in the right direction. Even so, my instincts told me there was something more. I dug a little deeper and asked her if she had additional income (other than what she expected from the proceeds of her reverse mortgage).

She explained that she received income from Social Security, and from a 401K which had dwindled significantly. As it turned out, she was living slightly beyond her means; not in any extravagant way. There was just, as they say, more month left over after the fixed income. Unfortunately, as a result of a steady drop in the stock market, she was eating away the equity and principal of her retirement investments, and she was concerned it would be depleted at her current rate of consumption. Her 401K offered additional income, provided funds for special expenses and acted as an emergency fund. This was the underlying issue of why Sandy wanted *and needed* a reverse mortgage.

Now that I understood the problem, my responsibility was to educate Sandy about reverse mortgages so she could make some decisions. I explained to Sandy that the best way for her to understand a reverse mortgage was to review three financial documents: the Loan Comparison, the Amortization Table and the Good Faith Estimate. Once I went through these critical documents with her, line by line, she had a thorough understanding of how a reverse mortgage works, what to expect, and what the costs would be. I further described what the reverse mortgage process looked like. I took my time and went over every detail - application, counseling, document gathering, and submission – and included a timeline for each step of the process. Sandy was prepared to get things moving immediately. She signed the application and the disclosures, but had some concern about whether she should choose a fixed rate or a variable rate product. She struggled with the concept that a variable rate product was full of unknowns, and that it could eventually consume the equity in her home if the rate jumped to the maximum level. I made it clear to her that at any time during this process, she could change the product and the mix of how she would receive funds. It was comforting to her to know that there was no pressure to decide the product type immediately. However, she still had a concern over her home equity and what was going to happen to it.

Sandy liked the option of the fixed rate, but she did not like that she would receive all of her available equity in one lump sum. She also liked the options of the line of credit and the monthly payment that variable rate products offered.

After that first meeting, we met again the following week to review amortization tables for fixed rate versus two different variable rate alternatives. Again, our meeting started with coffee and an update on family and friends. Then we spent almost two hours reviewing numbers, and again discussing Sandy's goals and objectives. We dug in a little deeper regarding the amount of money she was spending on a monthly basis. As the conversation progressed, we talked about the opportunities to increase her monthly income slightly above her true monthly spending. Sandy acknowledged that by increasing her monthly income by $400 or more, she would drastically improve her cash flow. She agreed it would give her a significant amount of "breathing room." The extra money would be a wonderful addition to her Social Security income. This supplementary cash would also allow her to build a reserve for traveling to visit her family. The added money would also give her peace of mind, and she could comfortably live within her means. This was Sandy's "Aha" moment! She now understood how a reverse mortgage could provide her with a sense of calm and comfort. She could receive monthly payments to supplement her Social Security and still maintain a significant amount of money in a line of credit. The line of credit would do everything that her 401K was failing to do. This was the assurance she needed to know she was making the right decision. The reverse mortgage provided the means to accomplish her immediate goals and also addressed two essential long-term goals, an increase in monthly income and additional money available in a line of credit as an emergency fund.

A few months after Sandy's reverse mortgage funded, I asked her to share her thoughts on our process. She told me that I did a great job in answering all of her questions and supporting her decisions. She appreciated that I took the time to educate her to a point where she could make the right decision, and she was happy that she made this decision. Sandy also told me that her reverse mortgage changed her life significantly. She no longer worries about cash-flow, about getting her projects done, or having the ability to see her kids that live several thousand miles away. The reverse mortgage made momentous changes to her life - lifting a great burden from her.

About Tom Ritter

866-672-5850
tom.ritter@axiafinancial.com
www.axiasls.com

Tom Ritter serves as president of Axia Senior Lending Solutions, a division of Axia Financial, LLC which operates in Oregon, Washington, and Idaho. He has been providing solutions to clients for over 24 years in the capacity of sales, market development and sales management. Tom served as the president and CEO of a Customer Relationship Management software start-up in the late 90's. The business analyzed sales processes and helped professionals communicate more effectively with clients and internal team members.

Tom enjoys living in the Pacific Northwest with his wife and five children and finds that helping his clients with reverse mortgage solutions is very rewarding. Please call him if you would like to learn more about what a reverse mortgage can do for you.

Chapter

34

Jerry Boyd
Troy Freesemann
Waterstone Mortgage Corp

THREE CIRCLES OF INCOME CREATE COMFORT

(Story told by the Reverse Mortgage Professionals)

At ages 78 and 77 our senior clients, Bill and June, were the perfect picture of health. After an afternoon of boating, they sat in the living room of their Wisconsin lake home and saw an advertisement on television that piqued their interest. The television commercial explained how a reverse mortgage helped seniors, and they wanted to explore how one might help them.

One of their concerns was that the property values in their area had risen so fast that their taxes had almost doubled in ten years. It had gotten to the point that they were getting taxed off the lake! Besides an increase in property taxes, Bill and June faced another common problem we see with our senior clients: They were at the point in their retirement where their assets were dwindling. They had between $60,000 and $80,000 worth of mutual funds in their portfolio but were concerned that they were going to run out of money. As it was, Bill and June were withdrawing $1,000 a month from their portfolio just to supplement their retirement income. Bill and June were healthier and living longer, so it was going to take more cash than what they had expected when they planned their retirement years earlier.

Unfortunately, in the six years leading up to exploring a reverse mortgage, Bill and June had actually lost quite a bit of money that was once in their mutual funds – both from taking monthly withdrawal and from stock market losses. That loss was really what spawned their initial inquiry and our meeting. They thought they had a solid retirement plan put together and that everything was going to be fine; however, the reality of it was that the huge loss from their mutual funds coupled with an increase in their property taxes created a different scenario at their age. We, at Moneywise, find this is one of the biggest fears that most retired seniors have – running out of money.

Bill and June's concerns were valid especially when you consider the tax implications associated with withdrawing mutual funds. Unfortunately, Uncle Sam would take a substantial chunk of their retirement if they continued the path they were on.

Our job was to figure out a new source of funds (other than their mutual funds) for Bill and June to tap into on a monthly basis. When we investigated their particular situation in more detail, what we determined was that if they were to continue to withdrawal $1,000 a month from their investment, they were creating a scenario where their money was going to last far less than anticipated. Uncle Sam would end up with at least 1/3 of their total investment.

Our first meeting with Bill and June was a lengthy one, but it ended positively with both of them gaining an understanding that they had options. They were still trying to get their arms around if this financial tool, a reverse mortgage, was a good one for them because there were some unknowns. This was new ground for Bill and June and they needed time to make sure it made sense for them in their situation. They expressed their nervousness with any option that included their home. They did not want to jeopardize losing their beautiful home at this stage of their lives.

After months of following up with Bill and June to answer their questions, multiple meetings with us (at Moneywise), discussions with their five children, and their attorney, the epiphany came for Bill and June when they understood that their home wasn't just a home it was an investment. I remember Bill saying, "Now I understand that this (his home) is no different than one of my mutual funds or one of my investments in the stock market. I now have the ability to tap into that resource."

Helping Bill and June understand that they had three circles of cash to live from was critical. To achieve this, we took out a piece of paper and drew three circles. The left circle represented their potential in a real estate account (reverse mortgage). The center circle represented their investment account, and the third circle represented their bank account. From there, we then drew an arrow coming into the top of the bank account and designated their social security and pension incomes. On the bottom right of the bank account circle, we drew a spigot with a tap on it. Below that spigot, we place a dollar sign. This is the outgoing money from bills, lifestyle money, taxes, and all other spending. This exercise helped us to explain the blended effect of taking money out of their tax-free real estate account. And keeping them in a lower tax-bracket to keep more of their savings in their mutual funds rather than transferring it to Uncle Sam.

Bill and June made the decision to use their home as a financial tool and three years later, their investment accounts hold approximately the same balance as they did when they first took out their reverse mortgage. They no longer need to withdrawal from their investments. Instead, they are only taking the growth income out of it to make up the $1,000 a month that they deservingly want so that life is comfortable in their golden years. They sleep better each night knowing that they are not going to run out of money. This reverse mortgage was the right financial tool to compliment their current assets making Bill and June's financial picture a lot brighter, so they could continue to enjoy their retirement years!

About Jerry Boyd and Troy Freesemann

866-800-0280
Jerry Boyd, Home Equity Advisor, CSA
(Certified Senior Advisor)
Troy Freesemann, Home Equity Advisor, CSA
(Certified Senior Advisor)
jboyd@waterstonemortgage.com
tfreesemann@waterstonemortgage.com

We have been in business for over 12 years and have specialized in Reverse Mortgages for over three years. Troy and Jerry are passionate about working with seniors and love educating people about the benefits of reverse mortgages. Our philosophy is this: If you share information with people and have their best interest in mind, you can provide the best service and make a lot of friends along the way. When you do something that works for people and improves their quality of life, it's a good thing.

Chapter

35

Kevin Reichard
Senior Finance Network

SENIOR SUPER HERO

(Story told by the Reverse Mortgage Professional)

I was sitting at my desk in my home office comparing two great job offers after me, my wife (Katie), and our two young daughters had settled into South Florida. I was searching for a new job to further support my family in our new home.

At that very moment, the phone rang, and it was my Aunt Eileen calling from Massachusetts. "I hear you are on the job hunt," she said. "Don't sign any offers to work anywhere until I come to Florida and spend some time showing you the incredible career that I have found for myself. I think it is right up your alley."

I knew that Eileen was doing something in the mortgage world, at Wells Fargo, but I had little interest in getting involved in the real estate or mortgage business. I replied, "I appreciate your help, but I cannot see getting involved in the mortgage business right now." It was January 2005, and the housing bubble was pretty big at this point (and we all know what happened in the years that followed). I was fairly certain that a career in mortgages was not a great bet at that time.

"I understand what you are saying, but I promise this is different." Eileen said. "You owe it to yourself to meet with me. I can assure you that it will be worth your while!"

So I did what any good nephew does and set up a long lunch meeting with Aunt Eileen here in Florida. This has since become a pivotal moment in my life - one that I look back at and wonder at how the timing, circumstances, and luck formed what is now such a huge part of who I am.

I sat with Eileen, and she explained exactly what a reverse mortgage was, how it worked, and why the senior population needed such a financial product. She also shared how she had personally experienced many instances of helping seniors in need, and in some cases, even saved their homes.

After an hour, she had me hook, line, and sinker. For the first time I truly understood what a reverse mortgage was. A product that allowed seniors to stay in their home no matter what and gave them access to tax free cash to do everything from paying off their existing loan to receiving monthly payments forever, all with the security of an FHA guarantee was unlike anything I had ever heard of! And no matter what, even 30 years later, if the senior owes more than the property is worth when they no longer reside in the home, their heirs are safe because of the non-recourse clause. And on top of that, no payments! At first, this was unbelievable to me, and I totally understand why seniors sometimes have doubts and say it can sound "too good to be true!"

The thing I remember most from the first time I was educated on reverse mortgages is my aunt's quote that rings true every day - "You will be a senior superhero." I had never thought before that I would be able to have such a rewarding career, but my initial choice to sign up with Wells Fargo's reverse mortgage team and become an expert on this special product has become just that, a true blessing.

Three years later as I am out walking my dog, I see my neighbor, Jim, out with his pooch as usual. Jim is one of those guys that everyone in the neighborhood knows and is friends with. After many friendly interactions with Jim over time, the subject of what I did for a living came up. That day, I proudly let him know that I am helping seniors by educating them on the FHA backed reverse mortgage products available as a certified reverse mortgage advisor. At that point, I had moved on to a local independent reverse mortgage company and forged a reputation as a local expert, dealing exclusively with reverse mortgages and seniors.

Like most seniors, Jim and his wife, Patti, have been bombarded with mailings and seminar invitations about reverse mortgages. In fact, they had planned on learning more by attending an upcoming seminar in town. Jim told me that he and Patti were going to go as planned and then would welcome me into their home and see what I could offer them in terms of a "good, fair and honest deal."

A week passed, and I found myself at their beautiful, modern, and updated home, learning all about them and their situation. The bottom line was simple; they had reached a point in their retirement years in which they needed more income.

It turned out that like many senior couples Jim and Patti had done all of the right things. They had retired with what seemed to be more than enough money to live in their home for the rest of their lives. Their love for each other was obvious from the start. Married for 50 years, the connection they have is something that was truly special to witness. They had planned to enjoy each others' company and take advantage of everything that south Florida has to offer.

They never planned on what happened next. Patti was diagnosed with cancer that needed immediate treatment. To watch them explain to me what they had been through was heart wrenching. Patti is a strong woman who has since beaten the disease, but her treatments had wiped out almost $200,000 in savings. This was the money that they had planned on using in their retirement years. It was gone in a matter of months, and they were now trying to figure out how to make their income work for the future. Their stress resulted from the monthly balance sheet leaving them short and in need of more income to live in the home they loved. They shared with me that their home was paid for so they had no mortgage payments, but Jim, at age 70, had been forced to take a local inventory job just to help make ends meet. They considered moving and downsizing and then decided to see if the reverse mortgage was indeed an option.

We discussed all the options available to them, and within a month we had successfully closed their reverse mortgage. They chose the line-of-credit option to access their cash as they needed it, and have been quite happy since.

I now share a special, unspoken bond with Jim and Patti, and it is apparent every time I see them walking their dog or when I drive past home. It is a bond that I am so proud and happy to have. Hugs at holiday parties are real and special. For this, I owe a special thank you to my Aunt Eileen for her visit over four years ago that not only changed my life forever but also continues to have a positive impact on the seniors who I am able to help every day. Nothing beats being a "senior super hero!"

About Kevin Reichard

Certified Reverse Mortgage Advisor
Senior Finance Network
877-825-6320
www.thereversemortgageschool.com

Kevin's resume includes a current position teaching the Reverse Mortgage Class at Gold Coast Mortgage School located in South Florida. Working exclusively in the reverse industry, Kevin has trained dozens of reverse mortgage loan originators as well. He has become the South Florida professional community's first choice for accurate and timely reverse mortgage information. Kevin's passion for helping seniors is unmatched. Now operating his own reverse mortgage company in Coral Springs, Kevin continues to happily help seniors and their families every day.

Chapter

36

Randy Davis
Dollar Bank

ENJOYING MY GOLDEN YEARS

(Story told by the Senior Client)

I never thought I would be working at a golf course at age 76. When I pictured myself at this age, I saw me tinkering with my car, playing golf on a sunny afternoon, and enjoying my grandchildren. Instead, I have to work in the rain and sometimes even the snow. Pittsburgh gets pretty cold during the winter months, and it takes a lot of work to maintain a golf course.

Life does not always turn out the way we plan, and it seemed that lesson became more prevalent the older I got. My wife passing away before me was certainly something I did not expect. I also didn't expect to need money from my part-time job to supplement my Social Security to pay for groceries and medicine.

It simply costs more money to live now than it did when my wife and I were planning our retirement years ago. Plus having children costs a lot of money. Unless I wanted to work up until my last day on this earth, I needed to figure out how I could get just a little bit more money each month. I saw a national television commercial about reverse mortgages and decided to call and get the DVD they offered. It sounded too good to be true, but since it was free information, I figured I did not have anything to lose.

When I watched the DVD, it made a lot of sense to me. I started to believe a reverse mortgage might just be what I was looking for. I was unsure of how my particular financial numbers were going to play out, but I was interested in learning more about how I could get rid of my monthly mortgage payment. Even though my payment was small, it was the equivalent of what I was earning part time at the golf course. A reverse mortgage could be a good solution for me, but I did not want to work with someone on the other end of a telephone. I wanted to work with my local bank and someone I could talk to face to face.

Excited about the possibilities, I called my local bank, Dollar Bank, and learned that Randy Davis was the person to talk to about a reverse mortgage. Once I got Randy on the telephone, I requested to meet with him in his office. Our meeting went well, and I liked Randy a lot. He seemed like someone who I could trust and was knowledgeable about reverse mortgage products. I was most impressed when

Randy told me that reverse mortgages were a good solution for some, but he acknowledged that they were not for everyone. He further explained his job was to make sure his clients were making the best decisions for them, not the best decision for the bank (or for him). That was exactly what I needed to hear in order to feel comfortable enough to share my financial situation with him.

In reviewing my expenses, Randy figured I should be able to pay off my small mortgage, get almost the same amount of money per month as I was working part time, and have a nice line of credit to dip into for emergency purposes. Ideally, I would be able to pull money out of that line of credit every year to pay my taxes and insurance, and it should not deplete much because of the interest earned.

The idea of me getting a reverse mortgage was exciting. It would do so much for me. Since this was something I was pursuing, I told Randy that I wanted to get my daughter involved in the process. He agreed, which was also another reason I felt comfortable with him. I felt it was important that all my daughter's questions were answered, so she understood what I was about to do with my finances.

When I contacted my daughter and told her of my plans to get a reverse mortgage, she had some of the same initial questions I did. I was able to explain everything to her, and by the end of our conversation, she was encouraging me to finalize the process. She felt a sense of relief knowing that I would not have to work anymore and wanted me to enjoy my golden years.

With my daughter's blessing, I called Randy and said, "Randy, I'm sitting here on $200,000 worth of coins in my house, and I still have to go to work. It's time to use those coins so I don't have to work anymore." I got to work on pulling the information together that Randy needed to finalize my paperwork and made arrangements to meet with the HUD counselor.

I am happy to say that my reverse mortgage was the right choice for me. I have such peace of mind knowing my finances are in order. Each time it snows, instead of bundling up to work in the cold weather, I make myself a cup of hot cocoa and sit in my chair and watch the snow fall. Thank you Randy Davis at Dollar Bank for making my final years truly golden.

About Randy Davis

Dollar Bank
2700 Liberty Ave
Pittsburgh, PA 15222
rdavis581@dollarbank.com
1-800-344-5626

Randy Davis has been doing mortgages for 21 years. He has a real passion for providing reverse mortgages because he sees how it helps give many seniors comfort and peace of mind through their golden years.

Dollar Bank is the largest mutually owned bank in the United States with 48 branches and loan centers in PA and Ohio.

Chapter
37

Steven Brooks

A SMART BUSINESS DECISION

(Story told by the Reverse Mortgage Professional)

Tom is a well known small business owner in Vero Beach, and I have had the opportunity to meet him a few times at various local networking events. Each time we met, we'd talked about reverse mortgages and he always seemed to show some interest and asked a lot of questions. After one of our discussions, I mailed him some information to review - which is how our relationship developed.

Tom is extremely ambitious, and although he is over the age of retirement, he is still actively growing his business - which specializes in offering employee leasing services. Many of his clients are in the construction business, and unfortunately, the construction business has suffered the last few years because of the economy. Being an entrepreneur can be difficult, especially during turbulent monetary times.

Tom can relate to this first-hand because he's experienced a reduction in business. This decline actually prompted him to review all aspects of his finances. Realizing the pending recession was not going to go away any time soon, he wanted to be proactive by exploring new ways to reduce his overhead. He simply wanted to be smart about spending money.

It just so happened that while Tom was evaluating his finances, we saw each other at a business networking event. Tom asked me if I would meet his wife and him at his home to discuss how a reverse mortgage might fit into their overall financial plan. Tom explained to me that the idea of replacing his existing mortgage payment with a mortgage that he did not need to make payments on was very appealing. It would free up a significant amount of money each month which would have a positive and immediate impact on the cash flow for his business.

I met with Tom and his wife, and we went over the reverse mortgage program. Like so many of my clients, Tom had already done a lot of research. In addition to the information I gave him, he'd spent quite a bit of time researching reverse mortgages online. Because of the tremendous amount of research he did, by the time I met with him, Tom was pretty familiar with the product. While there is a lot of information to be found on the internet, a reverse mortgage is such an interesting product and can have some complications associated with it depending on ones situation.

During our meeting, we were able to go over the specific nuances that would affect Tom's finances in much more detail. Early in our conversation, I asked Tom and his wife if they wanted to discuss this financial decision with their son. I always encourage my clients to discuss this decision with their children. I feel it is important that everybody in the family is on board, unless of course they do not want their kids knowing anything about their financial situation, which is certainly an option. What I find is that most of my clients believe this is something they want to discuss with their children before finalizing their decision. Tom and his wife agreed to discuss this with their son before taking the next step which would be to schedule the required HUD counseling.

In a matter of a few months, Tom and his wife had discussed the reverse mortgage with their son, and he supported their decision. They'd also completed the necessary HUD counseling, and their loan successfully closed.

Looking back, this was not a super emotional situation. Instead, this was a solid business decision and becoming proactive during a financial crunch. Tom was interested in protecting their investments and maintaining positive cash flow for his business despite the declining real estate market in Florida. If he had not made the decision when he did (before market conditions went from bad to worse just a few months later), it is possible the reverse mortgage wouldn't have been an option for him. With the shifting parameters of the market, there may not have been enough equity in his home for him to take advantage of this option.

During a recent telephone call, Tom said to me, "You know, I really feel I made all the right decisions at the right time. I bought my house at the right time and I made the decision to do this [a reverse mortgage] at the right time."

Not only did the reverse mortgage give him the capital he needed to maintain his business, but it also allowed him to put a new roof on their home. They planned to stay in their home for a long time, and without monthly mortgage payments to burden them and the equity line from the reverse mortgage, they are able to make some renovations to transform it into a the home they always wanted.

The bottom line is that Tom was being proactive instead of waiting for things to get bad or worse. He saw that his business was down as a result of his clients' businesses being down. He also recognized the decline in the economy and appraisal values, and by acting swiftly, he was able to lock in his reverse mortgage to eliminate his payments. Tom really did make the right decisions at the right time!

About Steven Brooks

www.mytreasurecoastloan.com
772-559-2960
or toll free 800-642-3188

Steven Brooks is a senior loan officer with the First Liberty Group of Hometown Lenders. He lives in Vero Beach, Florida with his wife, who is a nurse at the local hospital, and his 12-year-old son. Steven is committed to the community. He serves as chair to the Advisory Board of the Samaritan Center for Homeless Families. He is certified as a Reverse Mortgage Specialist by the Association of Reverse Mortgage Specialists.

Additionally, he has earned the XCO certification, a prestigious certification that fewer than half of one percent of loan officers has obtained. The certification required the completion of 90 different courses and over 400 hours of instruction, with both written and verbal finals.

Steven enjoys working with seniors because he can help them avoid outliving their money by giving them a safe way to maintain their financial independence.

Chapter

38

Chad Jude
W.J. Bradley Company

THE ANGEL MRS. NELSON NEEDED

(Story told by the Reverse Mortgage Professional)

Every client that we meet is important and special to us. We believe in a grassroots approach to working with our senior clients. At the end of every meeting with a client, we ask if they know others, including family members and friends that either have a mortgage or are financially strapped. The story I'm about to share with you is a situation where we could help a client's friend pay off her mortgage.

Mrs. Nelson had spent the last eight years of her life "playing" with bankruptcy courts. I call it "playing" because she actually saw filing for bankruptcy as her only option to saving her home from foreclosure. When she first filed for bankruptcy eight years ago, she owed almost $22,000. She could not pay the mortgage because her social security income was not enough to cover the monthly payment after her husband passed away. She saw bankruptcy as a solution and stretched out bankruptcy for as long and as many times as she could. Eventually, the court told her she could not re-file again.

Mrs. Nelson now had a past-due balance exceeding $74,000, and the house was officially in foreclosure and was set for auction. In eight years, she accumulated $52,000 in interest, penalties, foreclosure fees, attorney fees, collection fees, and appraisal fees.

What made the situation even more direr was Mrs. Nelson cared for her disabled son who is in his 50's and lived with her. If she lost the house, where would she and her son go? What would she do?

It wasn't as if she didn't try to keep her house by calling the bank to speak to someone about her situation; needless to say all of her phone calls were being ignored. When she called, she'd be placed on hold or experience the endless "push number cycle" before she could ever talk to someone. In fact, she said there were many times she called, and she couldn't even get someone on the phone.

During our first meeting, I could tell that Mrs. Nelson had lost all hope of saving her home. She thought filing bankruptcy was the only solution, and that option was no longer available to her. The irony is that HECM reverse mortgages have been around for well over nineteen years, and she could have done a reverse mortgage instead of filing for bankruptcy had she known about it. By the time I met her, she was so sad, defeated, and discouraged.

We completed an evaluation that included her needs, wants, medical concerns, and condition of the home. In Mrs. Nelson's case, we determined that her mortgage would need to be paid off immediately. I remember when she hugged me on the way out the door. I felt a huge sense of relief leave her body. There was tightness in the hug that said, "I really need help and this is my last lifeline."

Mrs. Nelson made her appointment for required HUD counselling while I began the process of finding out the exact date of foreclosure. I also needed to make sure that the bank understood that there was a senior citizen involved, and she was working on a solution (a reverse mortgage). Furthermore, I wanted them to know that the only reason that solution had not been explored before now was because she didn't have the information. Now that she had the information, she's already applied, and my company had stepped in to ensure that the bank would get paid and Mrs. Nelson would not lose her house.

It took quite a few attempts, but eventually I found someone at the bank that actually cared. He requested I fax the necessary paperwork to him. He was unfamiliar with reverse mortgages, although he was willing to listen to me. I took the time needed to educate him on the process, and he discussed Mrs. Nelson's situation with his manager. In the end, if I could prove that I was legitimately working with Mrs. Nelson on her reverse mortgage, they would give an additional 30 days – a "stay of execution" on the foreclosure. Thankfully, they gave us an additional 30 days which gave us exactly enough time to have the entire amount paid off in full and save Mrs. Nelson's home from foreclosure.

After the process was complete, the amount Mrs. Nelson received after the past due mortgage was paid off was around $12,000. That gave her a bit of savings should her social security check not arrive on time or if the house needed repaired. This additional money gave Mrs. Nelson and her son a safety net.

On the day that her house was to be sold, Mrs. Nelson called me in tears, and said, "I just… I just got in a FedEx envelope and I opened it." She continued through her tears, "I had to call before I left to see the doctor to let you know that you are a man of your word. I can't believe on the day my home was supposed to be sold; I instead receive a check for over $12,000!"

She then proceeded to read me what she'd written in her journal. She read an entry from one of the mornings she'd spent in prayer with the Lord: "I send you out an angel to watch over you. You have always kept your eyes on me, and I have not forgotten. You're my child and everything will be taken care of."

That was the message she received in her prayers. As she completed her reading, I could feel the tears in my eyes. She saw me as the angel that was placed to hold her hand through that month - to get her everything she needed to keep her home, bring relief, and make the rest of her life happy, worry-free and also be blessed.

About Chad Jude

www.ReverseForMe.info
24 / 7 Free Information Line:
877-INFO-771 (1-877-463-6771)

My team and I help seniors with free information nationwide through a network of over 80 company wide branches. It's not about the money, It's about the Love. Information is available about everything from free counseling resources to one on one or group teachings about the ins and outs and pros and cons of reverse mortgages.

As a child, I was primarily raised by my grandparents, which is why I feel I'm successful in helping senior citizens with reverse mortgages. Every single person I deal with I think, "If this were my parents or grandparents, how can I help them?" There are many programs available to assist seniors, and if folks viewed every client with the mentality of "this could be my mother or grandfather that I am helping," well, you would do everything you could possibly could to make their lives better. That's what my team and I do everyday.

Chapter
39

Jennifer Hart, CSA

DREAMMAKER

(Story told by the Reverse Mortgage Professional)

A few years ago I was volunteering for a meal socialization program through a local church. My job was to deliver lunch to seniors. I love being around seniors because they are like grandparents to me.

Each week, I was assigned to the same group of seniors which gave me the opportunity to get to know them. There was one gentleman in particular, Joe, who, each time I dropped off his lunch, we would find ourselves talking at length about something. My weekly lunch visits eventually turned into coffee outings.

Before retirement, Joe worked as an engineer for a chemical company. His wife, who passed away six years prior to our meeting, was a philanthropist. She had done a lot of volunteer work with their church and other charitable organizations. Joe did not have any close family ties like some people do. In retrospect, I think my volunteer efforts forged our friendship as it was something he admired and valued.

Our informal coffee outings took place once every two weeks. Joe still drove so we would meet at and try out different coffee shops in our community. During our conversations, I learned that the one thing Joe always wanted to do was to play golf. His excuse for not taking up the sport was that he never had the time or the money to get professional golf lessons or the equipment necessary to properly play the sport. But when Joe talked about golf or watched it on television, he would get this wistful look in his eyes. He would even swing his arms in a fluid golfing motion while we were talking. It was just the coolest thing!

Joe was not a multi-millionaire, but he did have a few assets. He had a comfortable condo that was completely paid for which made me think about how he could use his assets to fund his dream of playing golf. He deserved to live the rest of his life enjoying each and every moment.

One day over coffee I broached the subject of a reverse mortgage. Joe had heard of reverse mortgages, but he reasoned that he worked too hard for what he had and did not want the bank to own his home. I quickly realized that Joe did not understand how reverse mortgages worked, and I would have to go through a major education process with him. Carefully over the next few months, I continued to reintroduce the idea of a reverse mortgage. I did it slowly and not in a sales fashion. My goal was to have him understand and absorb everything I was saying. I began by telling Joe about reverse mortgages – both the benefits and what could be potential pitfalls. Then Joe shared with me that he had absolutely no heirs. He was leaving all of his assets to charity when he passed away.

I asked Joe if he had some extra money in his life, what would he do? Would he learn to play golf and where would he most like to play? His response was, "Well I'd probably go to Florida, because I would enjoy spending the winters where it's warm. I would like my own condo and to play as much golf as I wanted to." He then added, "I could meet new people and make some new friends." Joe's eyes were shining as he dreamed out loud then suddenly announced that there would be no way he could afford such a lifestyle.

I asked permission to put some numbers together for Joe to review. A few days later I explained to Joe how a reverse mortgage would benefit him. The more I talked about the possibility of making his dreams come true, the bigger his child-like eyes became. He just could not believe what he was hearing! Joe began to understand that his life-long dream of playing golf in the sunshine could come true! By taking a reverse mortgage on his current property, and adding $10,000 from an existing savings account, Joe had the ability to buy himself a condo outright in Florida where he could spend his winters in warm weather and learn to play golf. It was not long afterwards that Joe was traveling to Florida to start looking at condos.

My realtor friend put Joe in contact with a realtor in Del Ray Beach, Florida who was extremely gracious to him. Joe purchased a charming one bedroom condo about three miles from a golf course and is as happy as a clam. He started taking professional golf lessons and calls himself "Tiger Woods in training!" Joe even met a lady on the golf course and refers to her as his "close companion."

When Joe is in town we still get together. I will be the first to tell you that his blue eyes sparkle each time he talks about his new life. Joe and his lady friend typically play nine holes of golf every day. Sometimes when they are feeling great they will play eighteen holes, but that's a really good day when both of them are feeling like teenagers. Joe loves the freedom of doing what he wants to do, and being able to do it outdoors where he can be in the fresh air and warmth.

I feel so blessed to have been able to help Joe live out the rest of his life the way that he <u>wants</u> and deserves, and I absolutely love making people's dreams come true.

About Jennifer Hart, Certified Senior Advisor
Reverse Mortgage Specialist

Telephone: 847-210-3280

www.jenniferhartcsa.com

Jennifer Hart, CSA, is caring and understanding of the needs of the senior community. Throughout her years of working with seniors, Jennifer has built strong relationships with many senior service providers and has developed long term relationships with many of her past clients. Jennifer conducts business using the following as a guideline: to help seniors optimize the equity they have built in their homes thus enabling them to live their retirement years with financial dignity; to have all senior clients experience financial peace of mind and security throughout their retirement years: To increase cash flow and enable her clients to continue to live in the home they have known and loved for years.

Chapter

40

Brian Cooper
iReverse Home Loans

MY FAVORITE CHARITY IS ME

(Story told by the Reverse Mortgage Professional)

At 81, Anne is still a sharp cookie. She is an artist - a painter and a photographer. She is single and living on her own in a beautiful condo, and just like the rest of us, Anne has bills to pay.

Anne was looking for a way to relieve the pressure of life's expenses; she did her homework and found me on a HUD approved-lender list online. At the time, Anne was talking to several other lenders, but ultimately she decided to work with me. She said there was "something about me" - she trusted me. I was able to address her questions and concerns in a way that she could understand and provided her with accurate information. I didn't try to "sell" her a reverse mortgage. Instead, we talked and, together, decided that this would be the best route for her to take.

Throughout the process Anne called or emailed me her questions and concerns. I was always prompt to reply, which she truly appreciated. In fact, we still keep in touch, and she has referred several of her friends to me - which is the biggest compliment that I can receive.

The reverse mortgage option was used to eliminate Anne's mortgage, pay off a building assessment for renovations that was costing her an additional $600 a month, as well as pay off her property taxes. The available balance was placed in a reverse mortgage line of credit. Anne response to me was, "It is nice to know that it is there. This is the best thing ever!"

Unlike many senior homeowners I meet, Anne was not worried about leaving her home to family as an inheritance. On the morning we first met, her comment (and direction) to me was distinct; "My favorite charity is me!" She was quite clear that this was *her* life; therefore she was only concerned with *her* needs. If she wasn't, then who would be?

During the reverse mortgage process, Anne had a friend who was a financial advisor that she wanted to confer with and asked me to speak with as well. I thought this was a great idea! I always encourage people to talk to someone they trust.

There are so many misconceptions about reverse mortgages. Bad information leads to bad decisions, and the worst part is when a misinformed advisor provides inaccurate information and a misguided life-altering decision is made. So it is always my pleasure to include them because then I know they are providing accurate information to our shared client.

Here are the top 5 misconceptions:

1. **I will lose my home or the lender or the government will own my home.**

   FALSE: You retain title; therefore, you always remain the owner of your home.

2. **My heirs will lose their inheritance.**

   FALSE: At the time of repayment your heirs have two options. 1) They can sell the home, using the proceeds to pay off the reverse mortgage and then keep the balance, or 2) if they want to keep the home, they can refinance the reverse mortgage into a traditional or forward mortgage. They may even be able to refinance to their own reverse mortgage!

   Unfortunately, there are some senior homeowners in the position of potentially losing their home. If that happens, there is no inheritance. A reverse mortgage can actually save your home and ensure that there will be something left for your heirs.

3. You must own your home free and clear.

FALSE: If you have a mortgage balance or other liens or judgments tied to your home, the reverse mortgage would first be used to pay off these debts. Car payments and credit card debt are not required to be paid off.

4. My kids are against it.

FALSE: Most adult children of senior homeowners have their own bills to pay and are not in a financial position to help support their parents. They would rather you get a reverse mortgage to relieve the burden of monthly bills and to have a better quality of life. Just ask them.

5. Reverse Mortgages are too expensive.

FALSE: Reverse mortgages are not cheap. However, the benefits definitely outweigh the costs.

REVERSE MORTGAGE vs. HOME EQUITY LINE OF CREDIT (HELOC)

Would you rather make payments or not make payments? With a reverse mortgage, there are no repayments to be made for as long as you live in your home. Also, credit score and income are not qualification factors; however, they are with other loans.

SHOULD I SELL?

There is a popular phrase called "aging in place." Most senior homeowners have been living in their home for many years. They have a lot of history there. They raised their children in the home; they have ties to the community; it is a place that they feel safe and secure; hence the phrase "aging in place."

Let's be honest. Moving is stressful and can be quite costly. Sure there are costs associated with a reverse mortgage, but they are financed into the loan. Remember there are fees associated with moving. A real estate agent usually gets at least 4%-6% of the sale price. There are moving company fees and fees associated with your new loan. Is moving really worth the aggravation when a reverse mortgage will let you "age in place?"

There are many senior homeowners missing out on an often life-changing program called a reverse mortgage. Some people will say they don't want a reversible mortgage, or that they own their home free and clear and they don't want another mortgage. The truth is that a reverse mortgage works best for those who own their home free and clear.

Many people think they know what a reverse mortgage is because they got their information from what someone said or from what they heard on TV or read in the paper. There is a lot of inaccurate information out there. There are even mortgage and financial professionals who call themselves "experts" who have no idea what a reverse mortgage is. The sad truth is that some people take what they hear or read from these so called "experts" as the gospel, and those are the same people who could greatly benefit from a reverse mortgage. They are missing out because they made a life-changing decision based on inaccurate information.

Please do not make the same mistake.

Please read Chapter 17 for another story about a borrower that Brian has worked with.

About Brian Cooper

iReverse Home Loans
Telephone: 888-616-2667
BrianReverse@gmail.com
www.reversemortgagetimes.org

Brian Cooper made the decision to specialize in offering reverse mortgage programs because he wanted to make a difference, and sleep well at night knowing that he is helping people nationwide live a more comfortable life. He takes a sincere interest and listens to what the senior homeowner wants to accomplish. Brian provides accurate information so that people can make the best decisions for themselves.

Chapter
41

Ansley Wallace
Evofi One

A MOTHER'S GENEROUS ACT

(Story told by the Senior Client's Daughter)

A little over a year ago, my family was changed forever. After the dust settled, which took awhile, the changes were easier to deal with, but it was a long road to get there. You see, my husband was in a catastrophic motorcycle accident that left him in a wheelchair, completely unable to work. After the accident, we went from living pretty well to having zero income. I was a stay-at-home mom and prior to my husband's accident, disability insurance was a luxury we did not have. Going back to work was not an option for me. My job now was to care for my husband by taking him to and from physical therapy as well as care for our children.

My husband was in bad shape. Despite going through multiple surgeries, he still has a few more to endure. But if we could live through three months of my husband being in a wheelchair during the winter months (him being six feet tall and me being 4' 8") while caring for two children, I knew we could deal with another surgery. Even with surgery, his ankle will never be the same.

The past twelve months have brought a lot of animosity into our home. My once strong and responsible husband is now unable to provide for his family, and oftentimes it surrounds my family with bitterness and sadness. But I am an optimist and truly believe that no matter what goes wrong in the night, we always have a new day in which things can always get better.

We are truly blessed with amazing friends, and we have survived for almost a year without any income. My mom was also there for anything we needed. Our friends are caring and generous people who went above and beyond for us every step of the way. In retrospect, my family might not have been able to get through that year without them. My family got by with the basics and went without extras. We knew that we were faced with adversity and had to do what it took to hold it together, to keep moving forward, and to focus on what we had. Eventually, it came to the point where my husband and I just could not take any more handouts from people. We had a lot of people to pay back, especially my mom, and we prayed for a way to help get our family back on solid financial ground.

Then out of nowhere, a miracle occurred. My mom volunteered to do a reverse mortgage in order to provide my family with income, so we could get our lives back on track. Can you believe it? My mom was willing to use the home she worked so hard for to help my family. In retrospect, I still cannot believe how selfless she was in making this decision. She had already been so supportive, and yet a year later she was still trying to find other ways to help us.

I'd known Ansley Wallace from Evofi One for years, and when my mom and I were researching reverse mortgages, I found Ansley again. I couldn't think of a better person than somebody that I trust and know to guide us through this process. When my mom and I called Ansley, she took time to answer all of our initial questions and did a fantastic job of explaining the entire process to us. After a few telephone conversations, my mom made the decision to meet Ansley and move her application process forward. Ansley and I drove to California to see my mom, and together the three of us went over the reverse mortgage paper work, explanations, and timing of the process.

While Ansley and I were at my mom's house, the appraiser was there and made us aware of a couple of minor repairs that needed to be done with the house. I have to admit that I was completely surprised because my mom took immaculate care of her home. But the needed repairs turned out to be minor. One such repair was a comical one. Evidently, at some point in the past the noise of the smoke detector beeping every few seconds signaling a low battery annoyed my mom enough that she had taken it down. We reinstalled that!

A few short weeks later, my mom's reverse mortgage was complete. She was excited about the results a reverse mortgage would have on both of our lives. My mom can now travel wherever she wants (and she has already). The reverse mortgage has also given my daughter an opportunity to attend private school. Plus, my children can go back to doing the activities they enjoy - like basketball and dance. I can return to work to start paying back some of our debt. My mom's generosity has given us a chance to breath for a couple of years until we can get back on our feet.

This wonderful gift has completely overwhelmed my husband. To this day he cannot grasp that she was so unselfishly giving to take out a reverse mortgage on her home for us. He has never had any-body offer him a gift like this, especially in a time of need.

My mom's kindness still bewilders me. She saved all of her life to pay off her house and now was able to take care of me when I needed it the most. It allowed us to stay in our home. Being able to do this is satisfying to my mom in so many ways which makes me forever grateful.

"I would like to say that never in a million years that I would think my mom will do something like this.... For [us] to share some-thing that she'd worked so hard for, ... I will always appreciate her. I will always make sure that my kids appreciate giving to people because my mom has always brought me up to give. The more you give, the more you're blessed."

About Ansley Wallace

Evofi One
702-951-9514
benelibra@gmail.com

I came to reverse mortgages because as I approached age 60 myself, I decided to explore the subject for my own retirement planning purposes. I have watched so many seniors struggle financially in retirement, and I naturally began helping them. Having lived all over the world, Asia, Europe, Africa, and all over the United States, I have found that while cultural differences abound, people have fundamentally the same desires – to be understood, to take care of their children, and to live in peace.

Chapter

42

Mike and Josh Borba
MLS Reverse Mortgage

A HOME-SAVING ANGEL

(Story told by the Reverse Mortgage Professional)

One day after returning to the office from an appointment, there was a message on my desk to call Mrs. Lumpkin. Apparently, she called our office and requested information about reverse mortgage products. It was my job to follow up with her to answer any questions she had. My initial telephone conversation was extremely strange. When I asked to speak with Mr. or Mrs. Lumpkin, the woman that answered said they no longer lived there. She went on to explain that she had just bought that house and moved in a couple of weeks ago and had been getting all kinds of mail and phone calls for a Mrs. Lumpkin and had no idea who that person was. Obviously, I thought it was kind of strange, but I made it clear I would not bother her anymore, thanked her for her time and hung up the telephone.

The next day I received a voice mail message from Mrs. Lumpkin saying that yes, she lived at the address, and yes, that was her telephone number and begged me to please call me back. When I returned the call, the first thing she said to me was, "I know you're my angel sent from heaven. I know you are."

That first conversation lasted almost an hour. In that time, I learned she was in a lot of financial trouble which is why she did not want to answer the telephone. When I initially called, she assumed I was the bill collector because her home was in foreclosure. Mrs. Lumpkin had refinanced her home, and now simply couldn't afford the monthly payment. She and her husband lived on a tight budget made up of her husband's retirement income and her disability. Since refinancing their original home loan, their new mortgage payment was nearly half of their income.

Then she explained to me that there was a gentleman that was working with her bank to buy her house out of foreclosure. Mrs. Lumpkin felt it was important for me to talk to him. I asked her why she was inquiring about a reverse mortgage if she already had a plan to stop her bank from the foreclosure. Her response was that she was desperate for help and needed a back up plan if the man did not buy her home.

I asked Mrs. Lumpkin to schedule a call with the man who was buying her home, and shortly thereafter she set up a three-way call between all of us. Mrs. Lumpkin's plan was to make sure the gentleman confirmed, in front of me, everything he'd agreed to in previous conversations with her. During the conversation, the gentleman agreed that he was going to purchase Mrs. Lumpkin's home for a mere $50,000, was going to allow the Lumpkins to rent the house back from him, and in a few years he would sell it back to them "real cheap."

I could not believe my ears! After hearing the ludicrous deal he was offering Mrs. Lumpkin, there was no doubt in my mind this guy was scamming them. He might fully intend to purchase the house, but I doubted he would rent it to the Lumpkins, and I certainly doubted he'd turn around and sell it back to them.

It was a good thing Mrs. Lumpkin called our office when she did because there was no doubt she was going to need that back up plan after all.

I needed to talk to my boss about this situation. After everything I heard, I got the impression the man Mrs. Lumpkin was working with was trying to take the house out from under her. I really had no idea how to handle this especially since I had only been selling reverse mortgages for six months. I might not have known exactly what to do, but I knew I wanted to be the one to help. I am not too far away in age from seniors myself, so I feel I can relate on a more personal level. My boss guided me through next steps.

My first step in helping Mrs. Lumpkin was getting the initial reverse mortgage papers signed in order to proceed and get their existing mortgage people to talk to me. Once I got them signed, I was able to speak to the person in litigation that was working on their mortgage. That person confirmed the Lumpkin's home was indeed in foreclosure, and their house was supposed to sell within a few days. My negotiation strategy to buy some time was to let him know that when the Lumpkins reverse mortgage closed, they would be able to pay the bank $71,000 of the money owed (and let the Lumpkins stay in their home) instead of the $50,000 the current buyer was offering.

Money talks! He told me to send him the paper work on the proposal. I faxed the paperwork over to him and he immediately approved it! The litigation manager stopped the foreclosure but only gave me until the 24th of that month to actually close the deal.

Thankfully, we were able to complete the appraisal, and we ended up closed the day that the bank said was her deadline. The Lumpkins were ecstatic. The house is theirs for the rest of their lives. Mrs. Lumpkin kept repeating, "I told you, you were my angel."

I want to be an angel for other seniors because I believe so much in the reverse mortgage and saw how it has helped a lot of people.

About MLS Reverse Mortgage

Mike and Josh Borba
13478 Luther Road, Suite C
Auburn, CA 95063
Telephone: 530-888-6000
or 1-888-888-4834
www.MLSMONEY.com
www.LearnAboutReverseMortgages.com

Thanks to our Loan Officer Jan Mondragon for her hard work and dedication to our senior clients.

Mike Borba started working in the Real Estate industry in 1979. Formally a chemist for Sunkist Growers, Mike became a Broker in 1980's and started in the lending business in 1992. Mike's successful and ethical business practices have produced many happy and repeat clients. Josh Borba graduated from San Francisco State University in 2002 with a degree in Business Administration and an emphasis on International Business. After graduation, Josh spent a few months in Spain, studying Spanish before returning home to open MLS Mortgage with his father, Mike Borba. Josh recently married his college sweetheart, Alexis. Read another story by MLS Reverse Mortgage in Chapter 11.

Chapter

43

Sylvia Williams
Sequoia Reverse Mortgage

SPIRITED 91 YEAR OLD
CONVINCES ME OF A REVERSE MORTGAGE

(Story told by the Reverse Mortgage Professional)

The power of word of mouth is how I first met Merle Cale, my vibrant senior client. Three years ago, she heard about me from her hairdresser and the hairdresser heard about me from one of her clients, who happened to be one of my clients.

Merle is one of the most extraordinary individuals I have ever had the pleasure of knowing. At 93 years old, she has more energy than I do! She has an extremely active social life and is either involved with or volunteers for as many organizations as she possibly can. Nothing stops Merle; she embraces life! In fact, it is not uncommon for her to get on a bus and go to Reno to gamble. She is always out and about, running around and having a ball. She is delightful, upbeat, has an incredible sense of giving. She simply is a wonderful lady.

On the recommendation of her hairdresser, she called me to inquire if I could help her. I remember that our first conversation was brief; Merle did not want to discuss her financial situation over the telephone, so we set an appointment to meet.

When we first met, she was about to turn 91 years old. I learned quickly that Merle is straightforward, matter of fact, realistic, and approaches her finances as though they were a business transaction. Merle explained she was a retired professional from the state of California with a decent income. The problem was that in her nineties, Merle had $250,000 in two outstanding mortgages due, in part, to a series of refinances she took out to help a family member. Merle did whatever she could to help others, even if that meant she went without herself.

She had enough money each month to make those high payments and have a little left over, but not enough to live in the style she liked. Merle was paying almost $1,500 each month for those first and second mortgage payments and was feeling overwhelmed. Her reason for contacting me was because she was notified that the first mortgage was going to adjust and increase. After the increase she would be paying almost $1,800 per month for both mortgages.

Merle wondered if a reverse mortgage would be the right solution for her. She confided in me that she casually mentioned the option of a reverse mortgage to her children who immediately expressed their disapproval of the idea. Instead, her son, a very successful insurance agent, advised her to sell the house and move in with him. Much to Merle's surprise, my response was, "Merle, you know that's probably a great idea."

I was reluctant to arrange a reverse mortgage for a 91 year old. I just felt funny about it. I did not know how long Merle was going to be able to maintain her independence, and because of that I did not feel a reverse mortgage would be the best solution for her. Instead, I suggested she talk to her family more and I turned down her request. She took the news graciously and thanked me for my time.

In retrospect, little did I know that she will most likely be independent for at least ten more years. The lady is that astonishing, but I didn't know that at the time.

For almost a year, I continued to talk Merle out of a reverse mortgage. One day, I received a telephone call from her. She informed me she was trying to refinance her house because of the pending adjustments. Merle said that she either wanted to do a reverse mortgage or wanted to refinance her existing loans but was unsure of what to do. I went to see her again. After some discussion, our plan was to explore refinancing simply because I felt she still might have to live with one of her children sooner rather than later. I did not want her to lose the equity in her home to fees.

It is important to note that I do not even do forward mortgages, but Merle had so many people calling her about refinancing her adjustable loan, that she turned to me to lend her sound advice. One gentleman, in particular, was extremely persistent and offered Merle a deal that sounded too good to be true. He told her that her payments could be lowered to $900 per month. I could not figure out how this was possible; the math just did not add up. So I called the lender on her behalf to investigate this "solution" further. While I don't work on the forward side, I know all the questions to ask to see if the solution they were offering was going to work for her. Sure enough, it was an option ARM (adjustable interest rate), and it would have put her in worse shape than she was already in. Now that we were completely informed, we crossed off refinancing as an option for Merle.

Over the next few months, Merle and I got to know one another quite well and began to spend more time socializing together. The more I got to know Merle, the more I realized she was independent and honestly would not need to live with her son for several years. Eventually, I felt comfortable in offering the solution of a reverse mortgage to Merle, and she made the decision to move forward with it.

Now, Merle does not have to worry about $250,000 worth of mortgages, and she has $1,800 extra money in her pocket each month. This allows her to maintain her independence, visit with her friends, go out to lunch, and even travel. If the reverse mortgage wasn't pursued, with the recent changes in the housing market and falling home values, she would not have been eligible for a reverse mortgage today and most likely wouldn't have been able to make those payments and could have lost her home.

Thankfully throughout this entire process, Merle and I have become great friends. In retrospect, I am so grateful that I was honest with Merle about my initial feelings. In the long run, I truly believe my honesty is what brought us together.

Read more about Team Williams in Chapter 20.

About Team Williams

Sylvia Williams
Direct: (916) 719-4683
Toll free: (866) 523-1959
Website:
www.reversemortgagetrainingsolutions.com
Email: sylviawilliams@comcast.net
My Blog: http://activerain.com/blogs/coachinginreverse

Robert & Sylvia Williams live in Elk Grove with their two cats. Both have been in the reverse mortgage industry for nearly four years and have originated approximately 700 loans between them. Both Robert and Sylvia are licensed Real Estate agents. Sylvia has earned her Certified Senior Advisor (CSA) designation. They are both committed to getting the word out about this wonderful program so that seniors can live their later years with peace and happiness, free from financial worries.

Chapter

44

John DeSantis
Delaware Financial Capital Corp.

LIVING ON FAITH

(Story told by the Reverse Mortgage Professional)

In spring 2008, I received a telephone call from Violet (Vi) Canterbury, a woman inquiring about an FHA program offered to seniors. We'd discussed most of the program's particulars when she stopped me by saying, "Praise Jesus! I have been waiting for the answer." During the conversation I came to realize that she was a devout Christian, and I'd soon find out that her situation was much direr than I could have imagined.

Vi couldn't see me right away because her husband, Ron, would be in the hospital for a series of tests that would last a few days. We set an appointment for me to come see her and Ron the following week.

Some folks claim they are Christian and talk about Jesus, and at the core of it, they are decent people. But instantly I found Vi to be an extraordinary lady. Born in 1925, she lived in a 1,800 square foot modular home she shared with Ron who is seven years her junior. Together they raised seven children, only two of which were their own. They took on five other children of varying backgrounds and race. Most were foster children and one was the child of a friend who had fallen on hard times. The Canterbury's lived modestly but had never once told anyone in need, "No." In my mind this is the definition of the word Christian.

When I arrived at their home, I realized the severity of Ron's various medical conditions, not the least of which was the ventilator he was attached to so he could breathe. The house was comfortable but definitely needed some work. It was hard to imagine raising the large family they did with such a limited space. The more I got to know Ron and Vi, I understood limitations in any aspect of their life was something they didn't worry about. These people lived on their faith. Family photos were everywhere, and despite his condition and obvious encumbrances, Ron couldn't have been a more inviting and warm gentleman. Unable to move around much himself, Ron was only concerned about my comfort. He wanted me to sit where I would be most comfortable and not concern myself with his proximity to the paper work. After fighting Vi and Ron off for several minutes, I finally convinced them to let me use a folding chair and the back of my brief case so I could be close to both of them.

As we dove into filling out the application, what initially seemed to be a relatively easy approval started to look a bit troublesome. Information surfaced that I was not fully aware of and was unable to foresee. Like I mentioned, after raising the equivalent of two families, the little house had seen better days. Then Vi showed me the mortgage statement, which had a much larger balance than we discussed along with some back interest. Between Ron's increasing medical bills, the cost of living and a modest fixed income, the Canterbury's were in trouble. I was then shown an overdue tax bill that only further evidenced this fact. When I thought things couldn't get worse, Vi showed me a letter from the electric company that served as final notice before being disconnected because they were that far behind on their bill. I immediately thought of Ron's ventilator, and started to sweat!

Just then there is a knock at the door. It was a young woman with an empty laundry basket. Her elderly father was the Canterbury's neighbor and had recently fallen. The woman was returning Vi's laundry basket. She said, "Thanks so much, Vi. Dad appreciates you doing that." Vi answered, "No problem." like she hadn't a care in the world. I was incredulous. Here is this 83 year old woman with the weight of the world on her shoulders, and she is washing her neighbor's laundry? Between caring for Ron, keeping up her home and fighting off bill collectors, she is still doing her good work. When she said "Praise Jesus" to me in our first conversation, I had no idea how serious she was. These folks needed this to happen in the worst way. Now I was in a panic. Could her faith pull us both through?

When the application was complete, Vi looked at me with the utmost appreciation, and they both thanked me all the way to my car. I put on the best brave face I could muster and responded, "My pleasure. No problem at all." On the drive back to the office, my mind raced with the thought of all the "ifs and buts."

The following Monday, the Canterbury's were scheduled for their mandatory counseling session. The day came and went, and I didn't receive the customary faxed notice that counseling was complete. I called the house but didn't get an answer. The next day, Vi called the office. She explained Ron had been rushed to the hospital Saturday with chest pains and an irregular heartbeat. She had been at the hospital almost continuously since Ron was admitted and apologized for not calling sooner. I told her that the counseling session could be rescheduled when Ron felt better. Two days later, Vi called me. Ron was home and with an adjustment to his heart medication, he was feeling better. As she requested, I rescheduled counseling (and then did some praying of my own).

A week later I received a call from the appraiser who told me the appraisal would be completed by the end of the day. I was truly worried and wondered how I would tell Vi if it came back with bad news, although I was sure she would take it better than me. I received the appraisal several hours later, and I cautiously took a peak. At first glance I thought it was a mistake because the appraiser valued the Canterbury's property at almost 20 percent higher than my best estimate. I immediately entered their appraisal into the computer - almost as if I didn't do it quickly, it wouldn't be true. Not only was there enough money to pay off the mortgage, back interest, property taxes, back taxes, all collection accounts, the overdue electric bill and fix all deferred maintenance, there was something else.

In the beginning of the process, Vi had in her mind that she wanted $11,000 additional cash from the transaction for something she wasn't clear about. I don't know where she got this figure because even when I initially thought things looked right, there wasn't nearly that much money left. When I realized that all of the bills these generous people incurred were now being taken care of *and* there was also just over $11,000 to spare, my jaw hit the floor. A miracle? I don't know. However, I do know one thing. If you live your life well, do the right thing and have some faith, things work out in the end.

About John DeSantis

Delaware Financial Capital Corp.
JohnDeSantis@DelawareFinancial.com
877-435-3388

John DeSantis first entered the mortgage industry as a loan officer in 1988 and has invested countless hours and energy into learning all aspects of the business. Since 2005, John has devoted his efforts exclusively to helping seniors through reverse mortgage lending and financial consulting. John and his wife are raising two children in Baltimore County.

Chapter

45

Scott Saitman
Reverse Mortgage Consulting Group

A FLIP TO REVERSE MORTGAGES

(Story told by the Reverse Mortgage Professional)

My senior client, Robert, was frustrated. The housing market began taking a major downturn, and as a semi-retired contractor and real estate investor, this was not good for him. For years, he and his son had purchased distressed properties or new properties and "flipped" them (rehabbing then selling) in the state of California.

Robert and his son had their "flipping" process down to a science. For every dollar they invested into a property, they would make many more in return. It was a nice business which generated a significant amount of income for them. But as the housing market conditions changed, so did their financial situation. Houses were not selling, and they needed cash or credit to reduce the amount of monthly payments that were due.

A traditional personal loan was not an option because banks were tightening their lending criteria. But Robert had an idea and went on a fact-finding mission to see if his idea would work. His idea was simple: He opened up the yellow pages and started to call the mortgage lenders listed. Robert had a specific question he needed an answer to: If he took out a reverse mortgage, was it possible for him to pay back the reverse mortgage and use the money again, like a line of credit?

Believe it or not, after speaking with multiple originators, he could not get a concrete answer. Not one of those "big" companies could even provide the answer to his question, and a handful of others simply told him no. Not quick to be discouraged, Robert continued to call and my company, Reverse Mortgage Consulting Group, was next on his list. I listened intently to Robert as he asked his question and my answer was "Yes!"

Naturally, Robert wanted to know how I was so sure that he could use a reverse mortgage in this fashion, especially after his experience with the other originators. I told him that I knew the regulation frontwards and backwards because not only do I originate reverse mortgages, but I also teach this information to real estate agents and insurance brokers in California. In fact, I have even been successful in getting two courses I teach approved by the state of California. One is a 3-hour continuing education course for real estate agents, and the other is a course I teach to insurance agents and brokers. I am really well versed in working with and speaking on the ins and outs of reverse mortgages.

I continued to tell Robert that certainly he could take out a reverse mortgage in the form of a line of credit and pay back the reverse mortgage then use the money again. He simply had to maintain a small balance in his account.

Thrilled with this answer, Robert began to share his story with me. In the good old days Robert had a rather large Home Equity Line of Credit (HELOC) on his house which he used to fund his "flip" projects. While interest rates were quite expensive, Robert and his son simply built that expense into their profit margin.

Unfortunately, Robert and his son were a little too late in their timing of this latest "flip" because the housing market started to decline. Robert now had a $3,500 monthly payment on his primary residence that was draining his finances. Robert had two choices: He could either sell the project for a loss or continue making the exuberant monthly mortgage payments. Neither of those choices was very palatable to him so that is why he started looking into a reverse mortgage.

For the most part, Robert and I were able to cover everything during our initial telephone conversation. Robert asked me to meet with him so we could complete the application and schedule the required counseling. Once the counseling was complete, Robert went ahead and completed the reverse mortgage loan.

However, there was one small hurdle for us to overcome. We could not get Robert enough money because the balance on his original mortgage was too high. This left him with no choice but to find nearly $50,000 so he could close on his reverse mortgage. This was a significant amount of money for an already financially strapped, semi-retired contractor. He found the money–that was how important it was for Robert to get rid of his mortgage.

Our meeting took place in late November, and Robert made it clear he wanted to close by the first of the New Year. He wanted to start the New Year off with a solid financial plan. We were able to meet his deadline and closed it on December thirty first- thanks to the title company that stayed open late on a holiday!

Nine months later Robert finally sold the property, and he felt lucky that it only took nine months. When he called to share the good news with me, we discussed how his reverse mortgage became a financial savor. The reverse mortgage eliminated the hassle of Robert having to make a huge monthly mortgage payment. Without the reverse mortgage, he would have had no choice but to make a bad business decision. He would have had to sell the investment property for a lot less money than he actually sold it for nine months later.

This was a win-win for Robert because he was able to keep the property, maximize his profit, and not have to make a bad decision based on a financial problem. Robert and his son now have a quarter of a million dollars to invest in more properties which, despite the poor economic housing market, is exactly what they intend to do.

I actually use Robert's story when I talk to real estate agents and while teaching my classes. His situation illustrates to them that a reverse mortgage can be used in a variety of ways. I believe a reverse mortgage is a fantastic product that can benefit many seniors by enhancing their lifestyle. But it is not for everyone. The best decisions are made by an informed consumer.

Robert made it a point to be an informed consumer by doing his homework. I am thankful Robert continued calling originators despite his frustrating experience and I thoroughly enjoyed working with him.

About Scott Saitman

Reverse Mortgage Consulting Group
916 834-1864
Scott@getreversemortgageinfo.com

My name is Scott Saitman and I specialize in helping seniors enhance their lifestyle using the equity in their homes. I own a consulting company, Reverse Mortgage Consulting Group, whose primary concern is the enhancement of senior's lives. My background is in business with a MBA in finance. I am a licensed real estate broker and mortgage broker.

My team has helped many local seniors enhance their lifestyles and secure their futures with a Reverse Mortgage. With my weekly radio show, "The Reverse Mortgage Radio Show" I am able to reach thousands of seniors with information about reverse mortgages and other senior related topics in a fun and enlightening format. I tell you this not to impress you but instead to impress upon you my dedication to educating seniors about Reverse Mortgages. Many of my past clients refer to me as their "Guardian Angel" as I have helped them stay in their homes under adverse financial circumstances. I live and work in Latrobe, California. I've been married to Janet for the past 25 years and have 3 great kids: Alec, 22, Samantha, 20 and Hannah, 10.

Chapter

46

James A. Jones
Reliant Mortgage Company

NAVIGATING THROUGH AN EMOTIONALLY FROZEN STATE

(Story told by the Reverse Mortgage Professional)

I met this particular senior client through an accountant who had received informational mailings from me periodically. I spoke to him a couple of years ago, and he said, "I don't believe in reverse mortgages," and then went into an explanation of why he thought they were bad. As with many advisers who haven't had the opportunity to help a client with a reverse mortgage, he had many misperceptions.

One day, he called me out of the blue and asked, "Hey, do you remember me? I am the guy that hung up on you a couple of years ago!" We had a good a laugh about it, and then he told me that he thought he had a customer that could really use my help with a reverse mortgage.

When I met 80 year old Barbara, she was facing foreclosure in less than three weeks. Barbara just plain ran out of money. Her savings account had been depleted, and she could not afford to pay the mortgage anymore. The bank was notified as well that she was behind on her property taxes and that she no longer had a valid homeowners' insurance policy.

The first meeting at Barbara's home involved the accountant, a bank representative and me. At this meeting, Barbara was in an emotionally frozen state like so many of my clients in this situation. Barbara kept thinking that the problem was somehow going to fix itself, and she had not planned for any kind of solution. She was skeptical about the reverse mortgage solution being presented by her accountant and me, yet she also didn't want to deal with the bank. Barbara's sister was also at our meeting, who, like the accountant and myself, was determined to help Barbara save her home. Her sister understood the solution we were recommending and encouraged Barbara to keep an open mind because as she said, "Barbara this makes sense". Barbara, who was completely overwhelmed, sat wringing her hands not knowing what to do to save her home. She was so frozen by fear; she simply could not process any information.

To add to the complication, I also had to educate the local bank representative about the reverse mortgage process. Unfortunately, the banker was just as skeptical as Barbara. His bank did not offer reverse mortgage products, and based on the little he'd heard about them, he had already made up his mind that he did not like them. Thankfully, the accountant continued to remind the bank that this solution would work, and the bank would receive 100cents on the dollar this way. The reality was that the home was valued at $400,000 and Barbara only owed $160,000, so there was a fair amount of equity on the home. She would only lose it all if we couldn't convince her and the banker that a reverse mortgage was a viable solution.

Ultimately, Barbara agreed to complete counseling and sign the application. I convinced the banker to present this solution to the bank's board of directors for approval. He agreed only once he finally understood the bank was going to get every dollar owed to them by approving the reverse mortgage.

Days after the application was completed, Barbara took a bad fall and had to go into the hospital. Barbara broke her hip and her wrist which required surgery, and she didn't have health insurance. There was no doubt Barbara really needed money. Not only was she going to lose her house, but she also could not afford to pay her medical bills.

The bank got back to me within a week. Barbara's fall was a blessing in disguise. When they found out that she had fallen, they felt they had no choice but to approve the recommendation. They didn't want to end up with a negative headline in the newspaper implying that their bank was unfriendly to a senior. With the help of Barbara's sister and the accountant, we were able to pull together most of the necessary paperwork while Barbara was in the hospital. I met the appraiser at Barbara's home, which was after a snow storm, so I shoveled the driveway and sidewalk so Barbara's sister and the appraiser could get into the home and complete the appraisal.

After that the progression was smooth, and the lender even put a rush on this loan which took only two weeks. We did the closing in the nursing home where Barbara was recovering. I experienced an epiphany when I was walking through the nursing home to meet Barbara. I lost my grandparents years ago, so I had not visited a nursing home in probably 30 years. As I walked through the halls of the nursing home, I became depressed. It was just horrible. For me, I saw these older people as someone's Mom, or Grand mom. Their eyes lit up as I walked by; they were really lonely.

It was a sad experience for me to witness, but it also made me keenly aware that I was keeping Barbara from permanently living in a nursing home. She could now live in her home indefinitely. She could now afford homeowners insurance, health insurance and in-home care in order to go on with her life.

Because of this experience, I founded the Massachusetts Aging at Home Foundation. The Foundation is a network of professionals in our respective industries that offer free advice and strategies on how to help keep seniors in their home as well as help keep as much of their assets in the family as possible.

About James A. Jones

President - Reverse Mortgage Division
Reliant Mortgage Company
978-279-9391 978-500-5791
jjones@reliantloan.com

James has 25 years experience advising seniors and retirees structure their financial, financing and legal needs. Along with a graduate degree in Finance from Harvard University and multiple professional certifications, he brings an educational yet compassionate side to what is, often times, an emotionally-freezing situation.

James has been a national speaker and trainer well as a guest speaker on New England Cable Network, WRKO Talk Radio, the Massachusetts Financial Planning Association, the Massachusetts Estate Planning Council, Long Term Care Training Institute, and hundreds of town senior centers.

James lives in Boxford Massachusetts with his wife Jill and three golden retrievers.

Chapter

47

David Vincent Vogel Thais
Wisdom Financial Services, Inc.

A CHERISHED HOME PROTECTED

(Story told by the Reverse Mortgage Professional)

Believe it or not, I actually met my senior client, Carol, thanks to a referral from someone that was not my customer. This non-client had signed pre-disclosures with another company but still responded to one of my direct mail pieces. She was a sweet lady who was handling a reverse mortgage for her mother and needed answers to her questions. The lending company she was working with did not answer her questions to her satisfaction and starting her mother's loan process with me all over again was not an option. She simply did not want to start the process all over. Still, she had questions so even though we were unable to work together I took my time to answer all of her questions.

Over a period of a week my non-client called me with numerous questions, and at the end of one conversation, she said, "You know what? A friend of mine needs a reverse mortgage also. I am more comfortable referring her to you than the company I'm doing business with." That's how I met my senior client, Carol.

Once I received Carol's information, I immediately called her, and we had a long conversation about her situation. I did my best to make her feel at ease – allowing her to feel comfortable knowing that I was the guy that she (like her friend) could always call with questions. My philosophy is not to pressure anyone into a "sale." Instead, I try to have an easy conversation with potential clients and listen to their needs. With Carol, I made it clear that no matter what decisions she made, those decisions simply needed to be the right ones for her. As it turned out, Carol was in a situation where she was extremely stressed and wanted to get her reverse mortgage closed as quickly as possible.

Carol's source of stress came from unfortunate predicament. Two years ago while she was getting her car serviced by the local mechanic, a terrible situation occurred. She took her dog with her that day (which she often did). While waiting for her car, she and her companion sat outside in the sunshine. A mailman passed by them, and Carol's dog lunged and barked at him. The dog was on a leash and did not touch the mailman; however, the mailman was startled by the dog and fell over while trying to back away. Because of the tumble, the mailman felt he had a legal case to sue Carol and found a lawyer who agreed.

As a result, Carol was faced with a huge lawsuit. She had no idea how much legal fees would be or even how much it would cost to settle the lawsuit. Legal fees plus the fear of losing her home – her only asset – consumed her. Carol worked hard and owned her San Juan Capistrano condominium free and clear. She lived in a close knit community in the hills that overlooks the Pacific Ocean. It was her dream home, and she cherished it.

The reality was that this mailman had the potential of taking everything from Carol even though his tumble didn't result in any injuries. Carol didn't have the means to settle her legal dilemma, and she needed to figure out a way to protect her home worth almost $750,000. To add to the stress, she could not afford the "right" attorney, and the entire situation was becoming too overwhelming for her. This incident had been an uphill battle from the beginning. Dealing with attorneys and paying high legal bills was taking a major toll on her finances.

She heard a little bit about reverse mortgages from her friend that referred me to her and decided it was an avenue that she wanted to explore. She wanted to erase the fear of losing her home and knew that she had the ability to make this nightmare go away with a reverse mortgage.

Once Carol and I spoke, there was no doubt a reverse mortgage would be the right solution for her. Time was not on her side as she needed to have her finances in place before the case settled. To speed up the process, the vast majority of our conversations took place over the telephone. I did meet with her at her home when she signed the pre-disclosure, but that was the first time I met face-to-face with her. Each of my clients prefers to interact and communicate in different ways. I do my best to customize my approach for each client to meet their needs.

Within thirty days we were able to access the equity in her property via a line of credit. Carol did not have to take any cash; therefore, she did not have to pay anything nor was she charged any interest. However, the line of credit gave her the peace of mind that each time she had to write a check to the attorney or when it came time to write a check to the plaintiff's attorney to settle this case, the money was there.

Eventually the case settled, and Carol had more than enough money to cover the settlement. She was fortunate the case settled for a little more than $10,000, but she probably paid quadruple that amount in attorney's fees.

Since the time that the case settled, Carol's dog passed away. It was a sad time for her as she loved that dog tremendously. Recently, she did get another dog that brings so much joy to her life. Carol is an extremely health conscious person and having the stress of this law suit nightmare behind her has made such a positive impact on her both mentally and physically.

Interestingly enough, the friend who referred Carol to me recently called me and said,

"I have decided I want to work with you. I am willing to start the process all over again. The way you helped Carol was wonderful, and I just know you can help me too."

I earned her business the old fashioned way – by proving myself to her.

About David V. V. Thais

Wisdom Financial Services, Inc.
www.wisdomfinancialservices.com
866-947-3662 x110
Email: dthais@wisdomfs.com

David Thais has been the consumer lending industry for over 25 years. He holds the title of Chief Operating Officer for Wisdom Financial Services, Inc. and prides himself on offering superior communication and service to their clients.

Wisdom Financial Services, Inc. is licensed in Washington, Oregon, California.

Chapter

48

RJ Santiago
All American Mortgage Bankers

NEARLY HOPELESS SITUATION

(Story told by the Reverse Mortgage Professional)

When I got into my office on this particular Wednesday morning, I listened to a frantic voice mail message from Armando. He stated that he was going to lose his house and that he was running out of ideas. He was calling because someone recommended he speak with me. I could tell by his voice he was an older gentleman and was very worried.

That message led to my first telephone call of the day, and boy, it was an interesting one. Armando was 68 years old, retired and lived on a modest fixed income. His home was in foreclosure and was scheduled to be sold in a sheriff's sale on Friday at 11am, only two days away. Knowing that we had at least a few days to make a small miracle happen and save Armando's home, I said, "Okay. I'm sure that we have a little bit of time. Don't get too nervous. We'll figure this out. I have to get more details."

I drove to his house that same day. When I got there and had a chance to look at his property, I realized this situation was going to be more difficult than I thought. Armando's home would need some work in order to pass an appraisal.

As I sat and listened to Armando's story, I could not help but feel frustrated. The people he sought advice from were part of the reason Armando was in this situation to begin with. He was told he had three options: sell the house to get his equity, file for bankruptcy, or try to get a hard money loan. All of those options would just continue to perpetuate his financial struggles, not solve them. One of the biggest issues ethical reverse mortgage professionals, like myself, face is dealing with incorrect information given by people who have no idea what they are talking about.

Of course, when I told Armando I could fix his problem, he was skeptical, but he realized that, at this point, had no other options. He was not ready to walk away from his house and did not want to live in a rental. He had sentimental attachment to this home. His wife had passed on and he raised their eight kids in that house by himself. There was no way he wanted to lose this house.

The same day, we went back to my office and got focused on what needed to be accomplished. Our first task was to contact the bank attorney and find out what it was going to cost Armando to stop the foreclosure. He needed $37,863.45 and had zero money in the bank.

On our way back to Armando's house, I reminded him that all hope was not lost. There were still a few things that could be done to save his home. He was scared, numb, and had almost lost all hope. He just kept shaking his head at me; he really had lost hope and simply did not know what else to do.

My staff and I spent the next day trying to find ways to get the needed money to save Armando's house. I stopped everything I was doing just to help him. I requested a same-day appraisal from a local appraiser and learned later that day that the house was valued at $385,000. That was good news because the payoff was only $129,724.50 which left $255,275.50 in equity that Armando could use. With a situation in which there was a lot of equity but no money, I was able to obtain a 30 day speculative mortgage for him. This loan got Armando's home out of foreclosure and allowed us to make home repairs so we could get his reverse mortgage in process.

When I shared my solution with Armando, he was comfortable with it. We wired $37,863.45 to the bank the day before the sheriff's sale and stopped the foreclosure.

Now I had 30 days to get him a reverse mortgage. The first step was to get additional money to fix Armando's house up so it would be in good enough condition for the FHA appraisal required for a reverse mortgage. The work was minor but we had to get it done, or it would not pass an appraisal.

Twenty days from the date I met Armando, his reverse mortgage closed. That day, we were able to pay off the first mortgage and the short-term second mortgage. Armando also received a check for $10,637.28 for himself. Plus, we left an additional $3,000 in a line of credit. I told him, "Leave it in there. Just in case you're ever in a real jam, at least you know you have an additional $3,000."

A reverse mortgage saved Armando's home and provided a 68 year old man a second chance at life. He could stay in the home where he raised his children and not have to live in a rental. Without that stress, Armando now could address some of the financial loose ends he had. He increased his life insurance policy so his children would not have to worry about paying for funeral expenses when the time came. He even did a few minor improvements to make his home more liveable and comfortable.

I am happy I was the one Armando turned to when he'd run out of ideas, and I was able restore hope in a nearly-hopeless situation.

About RJ Santiago

All American Mortgage Bankers
347-247-4600
800-687-7516
www.nysenioradvisor.com

RJ Santiago has been in the real estate and the mortgage industry since 1984. He specializes in working with seniors facing problem situations and foreclosure. RJ made the decision to enter the reverse mortgage business to help seniors in financial trouble. He discovered the benefits of reverse mortgages and how he could use this financial tool to help seniors change their lives for the better. "My senior clients are now able to sleep without the worry of how they are going to survive on a limited income. I feel a great sense of accomplishment when I can help a senior secure financial independence." RJ personally works with every senior client and is assisted by his administrative assistant of thirteen years.

Chapter

49

Anthony Libonate
Delaware Financial Capital Corp.

COMMITMENT TO CARE FOR AND LOVE FOR LIFE

(Story told by the Reverse Mortgage Professional)

In retrospect, this was the most emotional reverse mortgage process I have ever been involved with. When my senior client, John, was diagnosed with terminal cancer, he was told he had less than six months to live. With a $180,000 mortgage, he knew after his passing that his wife would not be able to make the mortgage payments. He was searching for a way to eliminate that monthly payment and get his affairs organized so his wife's life would be as stress-free as possible.

John contacted my office in response to a marketing piece he received from us. When he explained his situation, I knew time was of the essence, so I immediately began developing different financial scenarios based on our conversation. Unfortunately, the numbers just did not work in John's favor, and I had to share with him the bad news - he did not qualify for a reverse mortgage because he owed too much on his house. Believe it or not, John was very calm given his situation. He just kept the perspective of taking it day by day and was doing all he could do to get his financial affairs in order. It is funny how you shelter yourself in thinking something like this could never happen to you.

As luck would have it, approximately two weeks after our initial conversation, there was speculation from HUD and FHA of changing programs that might be in John's favor. Every two weeks I'd mail him information in anticipation of program updates. Once we knew that the updates would be approved, we also knew that John would now qualify!

As we suspected, the updates went through, and John was my first call of the day. When I spoke with him, I found out that he was working with another reverse mortgage person from Indianapolis. This did not surprise me, as most of our senior clients receive multiple marketing pieces from reverse mortgage professionals on a weekly basis. As a matter of fact, most seniors tell me they call three or four people to see if every one is saying the same thing before they decide who to work with.

The very next day after our conversation, John called to tell me he was extremely dissatisfied with the other broker he was working with. He started his reverse mortgage process with one agent and when John called to find out the status of his application, he learned that his agent was no longer employed. John was assigned to another agent, and that agent quit the next week! John was a bit embarrassed when he called me but still asked if I would be willing to work with him. We both knew that due to his medical condition, he needed immediate assistance. Of course I would do anything I could to help him, and I was at his house the next day to take the most emotional application I have ever taken.

As soon as I walked into his home, I realized the severity of John's illness. Oxygen lines were everywhere, prior to my visit, I had not thought of seeing him in that state. When I spoke to him on the phone, he merely sounded like he had breathing problems, not like someone with a few weeks to live. He had difficulty breathing, but when I saw him, he'd recently made the decision to stop chemo treatments because he didn't feel it was adding anything to his life, only making him feel worse than he already did.

As we sat around John's kitchen table, the mood was especially emotional. His wife kept choking up with tears while he was talking about what he wanted to accomplish. John did his best to put on a happy face given the situation, but he even choked up himself. He needed relief in knowing that if his reverse mortgage went through, his wife was going to be okay, and he would not have to worry about her anymore.

Our meeting lasted almost two hours despite the fact the actual application portion took only 20 minutes. I spent a lot of time sitting and talking with John and his wife, getting to know them and listening to their stories. John was such a genuine man who at the end of day was just looking out for his wife. He said when he married her, he gave his oath saying he would always take care of her, and he wanted to make sure that he did, even up to his last day.

This experience put a totally different perspective on my business, and what I do for a living. It reinforced why I am offering reverse mortgage products - I help people stay in their houses despite their current financial or medical situation. I do this by listening to them, getting to know them as people, and asking the right questions relating to their finances. I am honest with my clients and treat them as though they were a part of my family.

We were able to close John's reverse mortgage within two weeks from the date of our meeting. I spoke to him minutes after his closing appointment. He'd called to thank me because everything went through okay. John's wife would not have to worry about paying a huge mortgage and would have a significant amount of money to comfortably live out her life.

John passed away weeks after he achieved a reverse mortgage. It was almost as if he was hanging on until he knew his wife would be cared for after he passed away. The love for his wife and commitment to her was such a wonderful example to witness.

About Anthony Libonate

Delaware Financial Capital Corp.
22 Polly Drummond Hill Road
Newark, Delaware 19711
302-266-9500

Anthony has been a Loan Originator with Delaware Financial Capital Corp. for over 4 years. He specializes in assisting senior homeowners to better understand the Reverse Mortgage program. Anthony is so dedicated to his work and clients, that he will often travel several hours a day to meet senior homeowners in the comfort of their own home. Originally from the "Jersey Shore", Anthony and his wife, Amy, now make their home in Delaware and are proud parents of 2 ½ year old, John.

Chapter

50

Tom D'Ambrogi, CSA
Redwood Mortgage Service

TRUE RETIREMENT

(Story told by the Reverse Mortgage Professional)

For many people, "true retirement" is never an option. Most people cannot retire because they have to pay their outstanding debts that were not taken into consideration when they planned for their golden years. My philosophy and the message that I try to convey to all of my clients is that a reverse mortgage, if used correctly, can be the key to retirement and part of their overall financial plan.

My senior clients, John and Sue, felt they were fighting an uphill battle. At almost 70 years old, John still worked part-time even though he is a retired naval officer receiving a monthly government pension. Having to work and wanting to work are two very different things and

John had no flexibility in this option. He had to work. John works at a local marina and had been there for 12 years. Knowing that he didn't have a choice, that he had to work, was a source of stress for him.

John and Sue owned a beautiful single family home in the Annapolis, Maryland area. In addition to their mortgage, they also owed money on their home equity line of credit. With an outstanding mortgage loan of over $200,000 (which equated to a monthly payment of nearly $1,700), John and Sue were desperately trying to figure out a way to actually retire and get rid of the financial stresses in their lives.

John and Sue saw a commercial on television which prompted them to contact me. During our initial phone conversation, my goal was to give them some information before we even met. This step helps potential clients feel more educated and prepared prior to us ever meeting face-to-face. I provided them with a packet of information that contains an overview of the process, information regarding required HUD counselling, and the appraisal process. I also include a reference list of clients and encouraged them to call my references on that list. I gave John and Sue a few weeks to look over the information, and when I followed up, we decided to meet to discuss if a reverse mortgage would work in their situation.

During our first meeting, I was interested in learning what their monthly payment was, including taxes. In John and Sue's case, their monthly payment was $1,700 a month, but they also had to set aside $300 a month for property taxes. This payment was a big part of the reason John had to work a part time job. Based on those numbers, over the next ten years, John and Sue would have to pay out $240,000!

Instead of making the payment each month, they could get rid of those payments and put that money back in their pockets. Then all of sudden, having to work to make payments changes to working if you want to. This would provide John and Sue with peace of mind and the freedom to better live out their golden years the way they want to live them. Our first meeting ended on a positive note, and John and Sue had a lot of information to digest.

Their first step was to talk with their children and ask their opinion about a reverse mortgage. They all said they would support any decision their parents made. Then John and Sue talked to their accountant. The accountant thought a reverse mortgage was a good idea based on his research and the information I provided which they shared. Overall, he thought it would be beneficial. The only downside the accountant could see was the expense of the closing costs.

It was clear that John was doing his homework when a few weeks later, I received a three page faxed letter from John. It began like this:

Dear Tom,

Sue and I are seriously considering taking you up on locking in a rate, but first, I wanted to show you some numbers and get your reaction....

What followed was this: John had put down some numbers and sent me six questions that I needed to answer for him. John was looking at fees and was crunching the numbers. He wanted a breakdown of the good faith estimate and also the service set aside fees and insurance. One of John's biggest concerns was that he did not understand why estimated closing costs were between $15,000 and $20,000. What I needed to explain was that fees with a reverse mortgage are higher because there is mortgage insurance and there are some set aside fees. (These fees are all government regulated, and unfortunately, they are what they are and cannot be changed.).

I continued to go over each question of John's fax and made sure each was answered thoroughly.

Once John was comfortable with the answers, he and Sue were ready to finalize his reverse mortgage.

A few months after their loan closed, I received the following note:

Dear Tom,

Sue and I would like to take this opportunity to thank you for your patience and the radical way you walked us through the reverse mortgage process. All of our questions were answered most satisfactorily, and we are most pleased with the final product. Sue and I would most happily recommend the reverse mortgage option and Redwood Mortgage Service to all qualified and that you process their transaction.

Thank you,

John

A reverse mortgage gave John and Sue the opportunity to truly retire!

About Tom D'Ambrogi, Certified Senior Advisor

Redwood Mortgage
tomd@redwood-mortgage.com
www.redwood-mortgage.com
1-800-520-7996

Tom lives in Maryland with his wife, two college age children, and dog. I think we're in a state of big uncertainty based on today's financial situation. People are getting older, and they're living longer. Expenses are going up. Retirements are not going to be there and we will probably be seeing that more and more as this news unfold. People will be using a "reverse mortgage" as part of their retirement planning. Our goal is to help seniors enjoy life and plan for the future!

Chapter

51

Len Ricci
Real Estate Mortgage Network

SAVING A HOME WITH TEAMWORK

(Story told by the Reverse Mortgage Professional)

My relationship with this senior started when I received a telephone call from a financial planner I'd met years ago. He wanted to discuss his client's situation and knew I offered reverse mortgage products and had a solid reputation for helping my clients. My philosophy centers on improving the lifestyle and financial picture of seniors - exactly what he needed for his client. The financial planner explained that his client's property was in foreclosure and immediate help was needed.

The client's story was this: The client owned her home for decades, and about six years ago she started having difficulty keeping up with the repairs and property taxes. At that time, the client made the decision to turn the property over to her son. The agreement between them was he would allow his mother to continue to live in the home for the duration of her life, and she would pay the bills associated with living in the home, such as utilities.

At some point the son, who is self employed as a contractor, needed money to expand his business and obtained a mortgage on the property to use as a line of credit. When the housing market started taking a down turn, his contracting business also began to suffer, and he began having difficulties making payments on the line of credit. Eventually, he started making late payments. It got to the point where he could not make payments at all and because of that, the foreclosure action was instituted. When I learned of this client, a sheriff's sale was scheduled in less than sixty days.

The financial planner and I met with both mom and son. The mother was naturally nervous because of the foreclosure notification. In fact, she was so anxious she was shaking like a leaf. After all, this was the home that she and her husband had purchased decades ago and it was now in harm's way. She shared with us that she had not slept well for several weeks due to the impending foreclosure, and at 82 years old, sleep is necessary for good health. She asked me if there was any way to save her home because it meant more to her than anything in the world. Furthermore, not only was it her home, but due to her son's business problems, he and his wife now lived there, too. Obviously, the foreclosure was going to impact many lives.

What struck me during our meeting was that mom was genuinely not displeased with her son. She was upset with the chain of events and disappointed that he had decided to utilize the home, but she understood that he did not plan or anticipate the down turn in his business. In her eyes, he'd fallen on some hard luck, and the foreclosure was simply a byproduct of the hard luck.

Initially, the question that needed to be answered was whether or not we could generate enough money through a reverse mortgage to get the home out of harm's way. Secondly, we needed to determine if this process would generate any additional money that could be used as a safety net for them. Based on our initial calculations, the second mortgage that the son had secured on the home left them with only a $5,000-$6,000 cushion.

Another fear I had was regarding the fees that are typically associated with a foreclosure - legal fees, back interest, and/or late fees. Sometimes those amounts can change rapidly, and I was concerned that there might not be enough money to cover those fees. By the end of our first meeting, mom decided to begin the application process and secured the counseling to pursue a reverse mortgage to save her home.

Within a matter of days, the counseling and appraisal were completed. The appraisal came in only slightly less than the estimated value (which was good news). The process turned out to be a smooth one, and we closed within 30 days of our first meeting. This saved their home from foreclosure.

It was an emotional closing for both mom and son. She hugged both me and the financial planner numerous times. They were so happy and thankful that the home would not be a lost. At closing, mom even had almost $4,000 in a line of credit in case she needed a new roof or a furnace.

Mom felt at ease with her financial situation once again. She didn't have a mortgage payment, and she continued to receive both Social Security and a small pension. Even if she didn't receive any monies from her son, she was now able to pay taxes and maintain homeowners insurance with the income she received as well as pay the utilities. Mom was especially overwhelmed with joy because she could retain the property and stay there for the duration of her days. In addition, once the son's business improves, there is an option to make payments on the loan, since there aren't penalties for loan repayment.

This was a situation where a financial planner and a reverse mortgage professional could work together to save a client's home and position the client in a positive financial situation. The financial planner and I helped improve the lifestyle and financial picture for this senior and her entire family for years to come.

About Len Ricci

Real Estate Mortgage
1-800-386-3791, ext 3527 or 201-738-3879
lricci@remn.com
www.reversemortgageweb.com

Len Ricci is Vice President of the Reverse Mortgage Division of Real Estate Mortgage Network, Inc. Len has been working with seniors for the past 20 years. His first job out of college was with the Social Security Administrations as a Claims Representative. Later he began his banking and lending career and was one of the original pilot lenders for the Reverse Mortgage program in New Jersey in 1990. He has worked with countless reverse mortgage clients through the years and has continued to specialize in servicing the needs of the senior community.

Chapter
52

Jerome Wilkerson
Guardian Reverse Lending

WISH LIST FULFILLMENT

(Story told by the Reverse Mortgage Professional)

I received a telephone call from client I had a done a real estate transaction for almost five years ago. She was calling on behalf of her father, Ernest, who was 73 years old. Here's what she said:

"My dad is looking into a reverse mortgage and saw the ads on TV. The short of it is he has a home which is paid for and worth around $200,000. He has some savings, but with all this recent financial meltdown that's in the news, he's pretty concerned and would hate to touch his savings if he needed money. Anyway, he would like some reverse mortgage information to review."

Of course, I was glad to send information to Ernest and thanked his daughter for the telephone call. When I called to follow up, Ernest's girlfriend, Sue, answered the telephone and said, "I'm going to tell you right up front, I've got a friend that works for Wells Fargo, and we bank there so we're probably going to go there first."

My response was, "Well, that's fine. Even so, may I ask you, do you know if your friend is a reverse mortgage specialist or do they just work there and then would refer you to somebody else?"

Sue agreed that her friend would most likely refer Earnest to someone else. I explained to Sue that the fees and interest rates for FHA loans and reverse mortgages are set by the government. I recommended that their choice should be based on dealing with a knowledgeable person who specializes in reverse mortgages who they could feel comfortable and confident with.

Somehow our conversation turned to Robert Wagner and the Senior Lending Network commercials she and Ernest had seen on television. Sue told me what a big fan she was of Robert Wagner, and that he had starred in some of her favorite movies. Sue was thrilled to hear that the company I work for, Guardian Reverse Lending, is a member of the Senior Lending Network. That was all she needed to hear! Sue said, "Well, I guess we could meet you. I'm not really in the family, but we've been together awhile. Ernest will tell you that he appreciates my opinion and so that's why I'm kind of outspoken. You'll find out I'm a very outspoken person." I appreciated Sue's honesty and told her it would make my role so much easier to help guide her friend into the best option for him.

My first meeting with Sue and Ernest proved to be interesting. He was in a negative cash flow situation and very worried about the future. Additionally, he wanted some extra money because Sue wanted to remodel his home, they wanted to travel to Hawaii, and Ernest wanted to buy his granddaughter a used car.

They had their wish list planned out well, but they had no idea how to fund those wishes. The good news for Ernest was his home was located in the greater Austin area, which has been insulated to the declining home values the rest of the United States has experienced. As a matter of fact, that area was seeing an average of about four percent annual inflationary factor in values of homes.

Because of this, my recommendation for Ernest would be to set up an equity growth factor line of credit through a reverse mortgage. At age 73, I estimated Ernest would need enough money to supplement his current income for at least the 10 years plus money he desired for the items on his wish list. We also needed to factor in interest and fees.

I estimated the costs for Ernest and Sue's wish list to be around $30,000. I also outlined the out-of-pocket expenses he would initially incur for the appraisal fee and the meeting with a HUD advisor. Based on the anticipated appraisal amount, Ernest would have approximately $100,000 to establish the equity line of credit.

Ernest did have some bad news to digest. He had non-performing, dormant equity in his home. Because of this, Ernest would have to stay in his home for at least three years. Quite honestly, by not taking out a reverse mortgage and establishing a line of credit he would be losing money. Based on the calculations, Ernest's $200,000 home (according to your property tax records) would be worth, approximately 40 percent more in xx years, and that would put him at $280,000.

When I showed Ernest and Sue the numbers in black and white they were floored! They couldn't believe what a fantastic option a reverse mortgage would be for them and were ecstatic at how it would fulfil their entire wish list – and so much more!

Ernest and Sue chose to go ahead with the options I presented, and months later they are happier than ever. There was another small hurdle I helped Ernest and Sue figure out. He and Sue were considering getting married, but Sue was drawing income from her deceased husband's Social Security. If she married Ernest, it would jeopardize her income and she wouldn't be able to make ends meet. The good news was due to the equity factor line of credit, Sue's income would be less of a factor in their finances. They would need to explore creating an estate for Sue and for her home, and although she has children, when she passes away, the home would revert in ownership to Earnest's daughter.

After Ernest closed on his loan, I recommended an online discount travel agent that gave them the best deal on their trip. I introduced them to a wholesale car dealer friend of mine who gave them a great deal on a used car for Ernest's granddaughter. I even gave them the name of a contractor that Sue visited with and discussed fixing up Earnest's house the way she wants it to look. It was so great to see they now had a plan to fulfill everything on their wish list!

About Jerome Wilkerson

Guardian Reverse Lending
512-899-3063
www.guardianreverselending.com

Jerome R. Wilkerson (Licensed Agent) is a central Texas native whose family has been in this part of the state since before the Civil War. His great grandfather started a real estate company before the turn of the 1900's. He has received the American Cancer Society's National Honor Citation as well as many other civic awards and professional recognition. He has completed and passed the Reverse Mortgage Examination - Reverse Mortgage Training.com. Jerome works with his Associate Melody Bull, a Licensed Mortgage Officer.

Chapter
53

Anthony Libonate
Delaware Financial Capital Corp.

THE SECOND TRY

(Story told by the Reverse Mortgage Professional)

We received a call from Mrs. Roberts after she'd received one of our direct mailings. Our company, Delaware Financial, sends seniors informational pieces on a regular basis, and in retrospect, that one piece of mail saved Mrs. Roberts from homelessness.

When Mrs. Roberts called, she wanted more information about a reverse mortgage, and she thought we might be able to help her. She'd already been contacted by another company, but they had then told her that she did not qualify because of the condition of her home, the size of her mortgage, and the fact that she'd received a rehabilitation grant from her local county to fix up a bathroom and kitchen. As she explained all of this to me, I was a little confused because those things were not adding up. Since she lived within our local area, I had a good idea of what the value of her property should be, and theoretically, the value would be enough to get her approved. Mrs. Roberts agreed to meet with me so I could get a better understanding of exactly what was going. I needed to see the property firsthand, especially since the other company stated her home was not in good condition.

When I pulled up to her house, I could tell just from looking at the outside of the property that Mrs. Roberts did not have the funds to keep up with the maintenance of her house. She greeted me at the front, and we proceeded to sit down in the family room to conduct our meeting. I asked Mrs. Roberts for permission to explain the concept of a reverse mortgage. She agreed so we discussed her options as it related to a reverse mortgage. So much was still unknown about Mrs. Roberts' situation so I asked her to answer a few questions for me as she showed me around the property. I learned that Mrs. Roberts was widowed. She owed $93,000 on her mortgage and was currently behind one month on her payments. She still worked outside the home to help pay the bills. She also had a granddaughter who lived with her and attended a local high school. Mrs. Roberts wanted to be able to reduce the number of hours she worked so she could start to enjoy herself instead of struggling to pay all the bills.

While we were talking, Mrs. Roberts explained the other company to me. They were an out-of-state company that conducted most of their communications over the phone with their borrowers. That company did send someone to meet her, but that was when they said she would not qualify.

I could see why that other company told Mrs. Roberts she did not qualify. Her situation would not be an easy one to process; this oftentimes makes brokers shy away from working with a senior. Delaware Financial prides itself in its ability to look at the entire scenario and research the best options to meet the senior's needs. If there was a way to help Mrs. Roberts, it was my job to figure it out.

The inside of Mrs. Roberts' house was not in the best shape. It was a four bedroom attached house built in the 1930's with plaster walls and ceilings. Other than the kitchen and bathroom, for which she received a county grant, there had been no updates to the house. There were holes in the walls and ceilings where the plaster had pulled away from the lathe. The hardwood floors were in need of refinishing. All of her windows had peeling paint on them, and her master bedroom ceiling had been destroyed by a leaking roof. Mrs. Roberts was only able to fix the roof and could not afford to have the inside redone. We knew that we had a huge project ahead of us, and we needed to help her so she would not lose the house.

After our meeting, I contacted a local contractor who walked through Mrs. Roberts' property and gave us estimates on making the necessary repairs to meet FHA standards. Once the contractor finalized the estimates, I had enough information to provide Mrs. Roberts with her options for a reverse mortgage. I felt we could help her, and when I shared the good news with her, she almost couldn't believe it.

Mrs. Roberts was ecstatic about the possibility of a reverse mortgage and decided to complete the application and schedule her counseling.

Our next step was getting an FHA appraiser to her house to value the property. The appraisal took a couple of days, and those days seemed like an eternity to Mrs. Roberts because she called several times to ask if we'd heard news about her appraisal.

When the assessment finally came back, I knew that she would be extremely happy. The FHA appraiser gave the value on a "subject-to" basis and provided a list of items that needed repaired so the property would meet FHA standards. We compared that list to the list from the contractor and made a few additions to the contractor's repair list.

When I spoke with Mrs. Roberts and shared the good news, I could hear the excitement and relief in her voice. I told her to hang in there and explained that it would take a few more weeks to get everything approved by underwriting before we could settle on the home.

Settlement day was amazing. It was so fulfilling to see the look on Mrs. Roberts' face. With a reverse mortgage, we were able to pay off Mrs. Roberts' existing mortgage, get all the repairs done, and she still had money reserved in a line of credit that she could draw on if she needed to in the future.

About Anthony Libonate

Delaware Financial Capital Corp.
22 Polly Drummond Hill Road
Newark, Delaware 19711
302-266-9500.

Anthony has been a loan originator with Delaware Financial Capital Corporation for over four years. He specializes in assisting senior homeowners to better understand the Reverse Mortgage program. Anthony is so dedicated to his work and clients that he will often travel several hours a day to meet senior homeowners in the comfort of their own home. Originally from the "Jersey Shore," Anthony and his wife, Amy, now make their home in Delaware and are proud parents of 2 ½ year old John.

Chapter

54

Bob Weber
Robert A. Weber & Associates

THOUGHTS ON THE ECONOMY FOR SENIORS

(Story told by the Reverse Mortgage Professional)

Time cycles have a funny way of repeating itself. I experienced tough economic times in the early 1990's and also in 1933 when I was 9 years old during the Great Depression. My family resided six miles outside of Thermal, California which is south of Palm Springs (and at that time Palm Springs wasn't even a city). My family and I had to leave our farm simply because my parents could not make ends meet. No one was purchasing cotton or vegetables. No one had any money. My mother found a job 500 miles north in San Francisco with the Red Cross; however, my dad could only find work in Los Angeles, so I went to live with my grandmother. The Depression had a major impact on my family, both financially and emotionally.

The Great Depression began with a catastrophic collapse of stock market prices on the New York Stock Exchange in October 1929. During the next three years, stock prices in the United States continued to fall, and by late 1932, they had dropped to only about 20 percent of their 1929 value.

As you know, the media has been paralleling the Great Depression to today's economic downturn. I hate to say it, but I saw this situation developing years ago. I tried to warn my fellow seniors but few listened. Many seniors have been raising their grandchildren. They use their home as an ATM machine to get by financially.

As a matter of fact, it's been almost two years since I gave a speech to approximately 160 seniors during which I strongly encouraged them to consider taking the following action: If you have a need to fund medical expenses, to help your kids purchase a house, or simply to supplement your retirement and you have equity in your home – use it now.

Out of 160 people, would you believe only three people took my advice? I helped them meet their financial needs with a senior reverse mortgage or government reverse mortgage. Boy, do I wish the other 157 people would have listened to me!

Every day, I get between eight to ten telephone calls from seniors whose existing home loans are close to or even higher than the current value in today's home market. Since January 1, 2008, in the State of California home values have shrunk by 3 to 5 percent per month. I can't stress enough to seniors to not wait to begin the reverse mortgage process sooner than later!

As a senior citizen myself, I can't just sit idle and watch this happen. I need to do something and help any way I can. I've taken on the role of lobbying to the banks - to show them that it is cheaper to subordinate to a reverse mortgage than to have a foreclosure on their hands and no qualified buyers and a senior moved out of their home.

I've become quite the amateur networking professional. Just a few weeks ago I had lunch with the Real Estate Commissioner of the State of California. He and his staff are helping me gain access to some of the executives at the United States Department of Housing and Urban Development in Washington, D.C. to put some new pressure on these banks to do this subordination. I now have some communication with Sheila Bair of FDIC and two people in Congress.

I'm also advocating the benefits of being more involved to the seniors I speak with. I ask each of them to write to as many people as possible from the United States President to the Secretary of the Treasury and even to the persons at the department that licenses the banks and to say "Look, I need your help to get the bank to subordinate the shortage so that I can still stay here and make payments."

Interestingly enough, I send out about 300 letters a week to seniors educating them about how to use the equity in their home and lower their payments to help them pay their bills or plan for their future. About three or four people a week contact me to explore their options. Seniors are simply scared to make any decisions.

They aren't sure who to believe especially since the media is focused on covering the "doom and gloom" aspects of the economy. To make matters worse, with unemployment rates over 10 percent now in California, people are moving away to find jobs.

Unfortunately, I believe that the United States is once again in a recession. Hopefully, the government will see the necessity of infusing the banks with capital to help supplement the shortages to the seniors.

As of today Robert A. Weber is funding approximately two to four senior modifications using the FHA Reverse for the bulk of the mortgage.

About Robert A. Weber & Associates, Inc

Telephone: 1-866-338-5767
Email: bobweberloans@hotmail.com
Robert A. Weber, President

As a senior with over 20 years of experience in both the forward and reverse sides of the industry, Bob Weber prides himself on providing proactive financial services to his clients. Bob's ability to meet his client's needs is what gets him out of bed each morning. Contact Bob Weber for: debt consolidation, home equity loans, lowering your monthly mortgage payments, new home purchases, and of course – for a reverse mortgage.

Chapter

55

John L. Krajsa, Jr.
AFC Reverse Mortgage Inc.

MAKING LIFE EASIER

(Story told by the Reverse Mortgage Professional)

Since 2004, we have helped several hundred seniors with reverse mortgages. I absolutely love working with seniors and never get tired of explaining the concept of a reverse mortgage to them. I have probably explained the concept a thousand times to different people, and it is always fun. Most of the seniors we work with are financially healthy and see a reverse mortgage as an additional source of income to make life easier for them. That is exactly what my senior client, Phil, wanted to accomplish.

Phil and I met through a mortgage broker. Phil was aware of what a reverse mortgage was and wanted more information to see if it would be a good solution for him. Phil had done his homework and had even spoken to at least one other lender previous to calling me. Our initial conversation was straight forward, and I sent him a standard packet of information. Once Phil had a chance to review the information, I offered to meet with him at his home to discuss his situation and answer his questions.

From the first moment we met, Phil and I liked each other. He is such a lighthearted gentleman. As a retired college professor in his 80s, he lives in a nice home in a suburban neighborhood. While sitting at his kitchen table, I took quite a bit of time to explain the program to him point by point. Phil is a very intelligent man, and he asked good questions.

Our meeting confirmed he could have gotten along just fine without a reverse mortgage, but when he got into a car accident, he realized he needed a new car and did not have the financial resources to purchase one. A reverse mortgage would provide a bit of extra money for a car and would also help him visit his children more often than he had without worrying about travel costs. He did not want his children to worry about him, especially his financial situation. As it was, his daughter wanted him to sell his house and move in with her, but he was not interested in leaving his hometown. He likes his neighborhood and his whole social circle revolves around the people that live nearby. If he left his home, he would lose that. As I do with all of my clients, I encouraged him to talk to his children about this decision because it affects everybody. Phil's children live throughout the United States but one of his sons was able to review all of the information we gave him, and he came back with two key questions.

The first question was, "Why do the costs of this reverse mortgage seem so high?" I explained to him that FHA insured reverse mortgages have closing costs that are higher than conventional loans because they include an FHA mortgage insurance premium, but FHA allows these costs to be financed and more importantly, that in many reverse mortgages the closing costs are offset by reasonable interest rates over time, resulting in a total cost that can be quite affordable.

The rate at the time of Phil's application was 2.25 percent, which was 2 percent under the published prime rate. The claim that a reverse mortgage is expensive is only true if you were to move out of your home within a short period of time. Therefore, the longer you live in your home the more cost effective a reverse mortgage becomes. To further explain the loan cost, the federal government has developed the Total Annual Loan Cost Rate or "TALC" disclosure which is a Truth in Lending Act disclosure promulgated under Federal Reserve Regulation Z (and is analogous to the Annual Percentage Rate (APR) also promulgated under Regulation Z for "forward" loans). TALC rates estimate the total cost of the loan, taking into account ALL costs including closing costs and interest rates and other fees, over time.

Phil's son reviewed the TALC (Total Annual Loan Cost) disclosure for Phil's reverse mortgage and understood the longer his Dad kept his reverse mortgage, the lower the annual cost was projected to be.

The second question was, "Is it best to wait until you are older because you will get more money? The truthful answer is that nobody knows, because the amount of money available from an FHA insured reverse mortgage involves two major factors in addition to age, home value and interest rates. It is true that with all other factors being equal, a person age 75 will qualify for more money than a person age 70 on a given day, but that does not mean we can promise a 70 year old that they will get more money at age 75. If rates go up or home values go down, you could easily qualify for less money at an older age, and anyone promising otherwise is making a promise they may not be able to keep. In Phil's case, he needed a new car, and so for Phil, now was the time. One major additional bonus was Phil decided to also use his reverse mortgage to pay off his $92,000 conventional mortgage with an $800 monthly payment; thereby he was able to eliminate his mortgage payment.

After Phil's children's questions were answered and they understood the program, they were all onboard with their dad's decision.

Phil's entire reverse mortgage process went smoothly. When his reverse mortgage was closed, it saved him the $800 per month mortgage payment which would amount to a cash flow improvement of about $10,000 a year or $120,000 in 10 years. This is a huge amount of money that Phil is retaining over time that he would be spending on mortgage payments, plus he has over $70,000 still available on his credit line and a new car.

Phil calls regularly and tells us how great his reverse mortgage is. He is excited about having done his reverse mortgage and believes he took advantage of something that a lot of other people just do not understand. He is excited about his decision that made his life easier. Phil's children are happy too because their Dad is financially secure and they can now focus on their own families.

About John L. Krajsa, Jr.

AFC Reverse Mortgage Inc.
610-437-7230 or toll-free 888-821-4076
www.afcreversemortgage.com

John L Krajsa, Jr. is president and principal owner of AFC Reverse Mortgage, Inc., a Whitehall, PA based reverse mortgage lender that is an FHA Loan Correspondent that is also licensed as a Loan Correspondent by the Pennsylvania Department of Banking. Mr. Krajsa previously served as legal counsel and as a corporate officer of AFC First Financial Corporation, a Pennsylvania mortgage banking firm and energy loan lender. He became a principal in the firm and was named Chairman in 1991.

Since 2003, Mr. Krajsa has focused on reverse mortgage lending, an increasingly popular financing program designed to permit senior homeowners to "stay in place" and improve their lifestyle by using their home equity for income.

Chapter

56

Thomas Eby
First People's Bank

HELPING AN INSPIRATION

(Story told by the Reverse Mortgage Professional)

This is the story of one of the first reverse mortgages that I ever completed. Since I was new to the reverse mortgage industry, I placed a full-page advertisement in our tri-county newspaper that was loaded with information about reverse mortgages. In those days, there were only a few companies that offered reverse mortgage products, so my advertisement really stood out. In fact, that advertisement is how I met my senior client, Theresa. She saw it and called me to learn more.

During that initial conversation, Theresa shared with me that she was 92 years old and had no immediate family. She and her husband immigrated to this country many years ago and landed in New York. They lived in New York until their mid-50s when they then retired to sunny Florida. She had some distant nieces and nephews that lived in other parts of the country but no one close in Florida. Theresa was married for many years, and her husband had passed away approximately 15 years earlier. They built a rather large home, and over time she had exhausted her savings.

Normally, I visit the senior clients in their home for an initial consultation, but Theresa insisted on coming to my office. For me, this was a scary thought because she is 92 years old and still driving a car! Despite my fears, she made it to my office the day of her appointment, and we went over the program together. Theresa's issue was she had owned her home for over 40 years and had run out of money. She said, "I'm out of money. I have to do something. I don't want to move. I want to stay here, so I read about reverse mortgages, and I think it might work for me." I could not believe how lucid and sharp she was at 92 years old.

I explained the next step of the process would be for us to sit down, in her home, to answer any further questions and to collect information for an application. I wanted to be sure that Theresa had someone else present with her during our meeting so I asked her if she had anyone who could attend. I offer this suggestion to all of my clients because a reverse mortgage is a fantastic solution for most but not for everyone. I am a strong advocate for ethical banking and wanted to be sure Theresa felt completely comfortable with any decisions she made. Theresa chose a realtor friend of hers to help her through this decision.

The first time I was in Theresa's home, I could not get over how large her home was. I asked her how she takes care of the house because it was so large. She replied that she does it one room at a time. Can you believe it? At 92 years old, she still cleans it herself.

This meeting was rather interesting because Theresa's realtor friend came in, sat down, and the first thing she said was, "Reverse mortgages are very bad. Theresa is going to lose her home, and I don't think Theresa should do this."

There were obviously a lot of misconceptions this realtor had, so we went over the entire program which took about 45 minutes. When we were done, the realtor friend turned to Theresa and said, "This is probably a life saver for you. I was wrong. You should do this." From that point on, we moved forward with the process. Theresa was anxious to get everything in order so she could live out her remaining years in her home. She chose the credit line option which allowed her to access money only when she needed it.

After the process was complete, Theresa tapped into her line of credit to make some general improvements to her home, such as painting and carpeting a few rooms. After the work was complete, she invited me over to see the changes to her house. And she does that each and every time she makes a change to the home. Theresa's realtor friend has even referred people to me so that I can help them with a reverse mortgage.

I stay in regular contact with Theresa, and she calls me when she has a concern about something. She receives a lot of mail from companies about refinancing that she does not understand. So I make it a point to spend time discussing how those offers pertain to her financial situation.

One of my most memorable moments with Theresa is when she called to thank me for a Christmas card I'd sent to her. She was very emotional because my Christmas card was one of a handful she received.

Theresa is an inspiration for me, and I only hope to live as long and as full of a life as she has.

About Thomas Eby, Senior Vice President

First People's Bank
(772) 559-0257 or 1-866-461-9383
tom.eby@firstpeoplesbank.com

Tom has been in residential lending since 1972 and began offering reverse mortgages in 2007. He received his undergraduate degree in Finance from the University of Miami, and graduated from the School for Executive Development from the University of Georgia. He is an active member of the Fort Pierce Exchange Club, a board member of C.A.S.T.L.E., a member of the St. Lucie, Indian River and Martin County Realtor Boards, and Treasure Coast Builders Association.

Chapter
57

Frank Melia CMPS (Certified Mortgage Planner)
Lend-Mor Mortgage

A TRULY THANKFUL THANKSGIVING

(Story told by the Reverse Mortgage Professional)

I was the kid you could find hanging out with his grandparents. I found them to be great storytellers and did my best to absorb the life experiences they would share. My love and respect for my grandparent's is one of the reasons I work with seniors. As a matter of fact, when I sit with a client, inevitably, a half hour appointment turns into two hours because they begin to share their life stories with me. I learn about their families, the favorite moments in their lives, and even the low points they have experienced. The story I am going to share with you is one which makes me emotional every time I tell it. I also use it as an example when explaining the positive impact a reverse mortgage can have on a senior's life.

Having been in the business for a little over 15 years, I have built many relationships with various bankers and financial consultants in the states where I am licensed to do business. I received a telephone call from a loan officer from a bank in New York about a couple that needed money to make substantial repairs to their home. The couple was retired and could not qualify for a conventional loan so the loan officer wondered if a reverse mortgage might be an option to pursue.

I gave the client, Dorothy, a call and set up an appointment to meet her and her husband at their home. Our appointment took place three weeks before Thanksgiving. Our meeting started with Dorothy explaining their circumstances to me. Through tear filled eyes, she shared that she and her husband received Social Security each month but did not have a pension. Her husband, John had been a self-employed contractor and never had a retirement account. When I met them, they had no more cash. Although they didn't have a mortgage, they only had enough money to pay their bills. That was it. There was no money left over each month for savings, home repairs or extras, including a turkey for Thanksgiving dinner. They were barely making ends meet.

Now they were having some problems with the oil burner which heated their home. Dorothy also shared that their grand-daughter had some health problems, and she didn't have health insurance so they wanted to help their granddaughter pay those medical bills. It was very emotional to hear her story and to see her and her husband so anxious.

When I explained to Dorothy and John how they could use the equity in their house to access cash to pay for a new oil burner and perhaps even help pay their granddaughters medical bills, she really started to get emotional. That is what I refer to as an "aha moment;" when the client realizes that a reverse mortgage can really help them. I continued with the good news. "Because we're a local community-based banker, our process can be completed very quickly."

We completed their application and the required counseling that very day. Once I returned to my office, I entered their information into our system and told my processor Dorothy's story and that I really wanted to help this couple. There was no way we were going to be responsible for them not having a turkey on Thanksgiving Day! My team got to work and had an appraiser at Dorothy's home the following day.

The house appraised well and when I communicated the news, I could tell Dorothy was getting even more anxious – not about the product, though. She was excited-anxious about the possibility of having the money to prepare a traditional Thanksgiving feast and also fixing the oil burner before the weather set in.

Communication was key with Dorothy and John. I made it a point to communicate with them every 48 hours; to just give them a call, explain the process, and reassure them that everything was on track. Within seven days from the day of our first meeting, my team had all of the necessary paperwork in our office and was able to schedule a closing. We went to their home and closed the loan sitting at Dorothy's kitchen table. They were very, very thankful for their reverse mortgage. Three days later, I personally delivered a check for almost $185,000 to Dorothy – which happened to be the Monday of Thanksgiving week.

She just did not believe it. I will never forget when Dorothy said, "I know I sound a little corny, but I prayed to God for help, and I met you."

I said, "Well, we're here to help." And it was a good feeling, especially during the holidays. It also confirmed why I do this for a living. I want to help people like Dorothy and John who worked hard their entire lives and experienced some setbacks with medical bills or home repairs. Those are real life experiences that set people back, and I have a solution that can help many people in those types of situations.

Dorothy called me a few days after Thanksgiving and asked me to come by the house. When I arrived, the whole family was there and presented me with a boxful of gifts for my daughter. They were all caring and loving people and were so grateful and thankful for my help.

Dorothy still calls me every once in a while and thanks me. She always ends up crying during the conversation and inevitably calls me her guardian angel. She reminds me how a reverse mortgage changed her family's life forever. They do not have to worry about money ever again. Between the money in the bank and their Social

Security checks, she and her husband can live in their house for the rest of their lives.

For me, the greatest gift was being able to connect with Dorothy and her family. When you really connect with people and see how your work can change their lives, it is amazing.

About Frank Melia, CMPS (Certified Mortgage Planner)

1-800-433-2120
reverse@lendmor.com
www.frankcmps.com

Frank Melia started his career specializing in retirement planning. After eight years, in 1998 he began working with home owners offering forward and reverse mortgages. In 2005, Frank became a certified mortgage planner, a designation which is held in high regard in the reverse mortgage industry. Mr. Melia primarily concentrates on helping senior home owners secure a comfortable retirement. He is licensed to conduct business within the following states: New York, New Jersey, Pennsylvania, Connecticut, Maryland, North Carolina, Florida, Texas, and California.

Chapter

58

Lucille Collazo
PrimeLending
A PlainsCapital Company

LIVES SAVED

(Story told by the Reverse Mortgage Professional)

I first met Josh at the local senior center where I was presenting information on reverse mortgages for seniors who wanted to learn more about the subject. After the seminar, Josh asked if I would be willing to meet with him and his wife. She wanted to know more but was not able to attend that day. A few days later, when I went to their home, Josh wanted me to know that they probably would not do a reverse mortgage. He said, "We just want information".

Josh and Barbara are a sweet couple. They welcomed me into their home, and we found we had a lot in common as we got to know each other. A few years ago, Josh and Barbara decided to move to a smaller town because they thought it would be a good place to live. They also believed it would be less expensive than where they were living before and they liked the community and friendly people there. They found a "fixer-upper" in their new town and decided to buy it and remodel it themselves. You might think this would be an awfully ambitious task for a couple in their 70s, but not for Josh and Barbara. They think of themselves as being young. And besides, they had built their previous home, so this was not a new experience for them.

Josh and Barbara started remodeling their new home using money from their savings. Soon, they needed a home equity line of credit. It did not take long for them to use up their credit line. They still needed money for completing the project. So they used credit cards. Eventually, they got a second home equity line of credit. When their home was finally completed it was beautiful. However, they were making two house payments now and payments on several credit cards. Josh and Barbara were getting a little stressed.

On that first visit to their home, I took my time explaining the benefits of a reverse mortgage and answered their questions. Throughout our conversation, Josh reminded me, "We're not going to get one, we just want information". Barbara would smile and say, "Yes we are". They gave me their information and I showed them how they could pay all their debts and not have to pay several pay-ments per month of approximately $1,000.00 per month. I wanted them to understand the impact this could have on their lives.

As I left, I explained that they could think about everything we talked about. And I also told them, "It is important to know your options so you can make an educated decision. I will run your options so you can see the actual numbers and see if it makes sense to you". I think Josh was happy because I also explained that there is no obligation at any time. There is a process including counseling by a third party and you can always decide if it is not right for you. Even after you sign your final closing papers, you still have 3 days to decide if you do want to change your mind. We set a tentative appointment for the next week and they decided to come to my office for the next meeting.

At my office, I analyzed their information. It showed how much money they would have available to them after paying off their substantial home equity lines of credit. Bottom line, after their debts were paid off they would have $29,000.00 available. Their choices would be: receive the funds at closing, choose a monthly income for life as long as they lived in the home or leave the funds in a line of credit that would earn interest. And, of course, they would not have to make monthly payments while their home remains their primary residence.

Josh and Barbara decided to go forward with the reverse mortgage and keep the funds available in a line of credit for future emergencies. They liked the idea of having a safety net and they were happy that they would also be earning interest on the funds left in the line of credit.

The next step was for them to obtain the required Reverse Mortgage Counseling. Any questions they might still have could be answered by a third party. When Josh and Barbara came in and signed their counseling certificate, Josh told me again, "We are not doing this." And Barbara, in her quiet way, smiled and said, "Yes we are". They applied almost three weeks after we met, and their reverse mortgage closed less than one month later.

I keep in touch with Josh and Barbara. They call me from time to time to tell me how the weather is in their part of the county, which is about 40 miles from where my office it. We usually have one snowstorm a year. However, this year we had three snowstorms in one week. Josh and Barbara had three feet of snow on top of their house on Christmas Eve.

When they got their reverse mortgage, Josh and Barbara were able to install smoke detectors and carbon monoxide detectors in their home. In total they spent about $1500 on all of the detectors. They also had a nice energy efficient pellet stove installed. It was nice and cozy in their home on Christmas Eve. Just before they went to bed the carbon monoxide detector went off, alerting them they had a problem. They realized that the vent on the roof of their house that lets exhaust (and carbon monoxide) out was covered by snow. If that carbon monoxide detector had not gone off, they would not have awakened on Christmas morning.

Christmas morning was also very eventful. Because there was three feet of snow on the roof of their garage, the garage collapsed onto their truck. Josh told me it didn't seem so bad because he knew he had his reverse mortgage line of credit. He could start rebuilding the garage and get his truck fixed. First thing he did was request funds from that line of credit so that they could begin rebuilding the garage right away and not have to wait for insurance money.

Josh and Barbara hand out my business card to their friends and share their story with them. They think it's great that they don't have to make a monthly mortgage payment. What makes their reverse mortgage remarkable is the fact that it saved their lives – both financially and literally.

About Lucille Collazo

Senior Loan Officer
PrimeLending
A PlainsCapital Company
lcollazo@primelending.com
Direct Line: 360-941-5220
Office: 360-419-0198
Fax: 866-557-7463

I have been in mortgage lending for over 20 years. My knowledge and experience allows me to provide my clients with a smooth, efficient process for completing their loan. More than that, as an expert in the field of reverse mortgages, you can be confident that you are working with a professional who keeps up with current changes. You will be informed of all the options that are available to you so that you can make the right choice for your specific situation.

Chapter
59

Joe Kiefer
Barclay Funding Corp.

JULIE'S EMPOWERMENT

(Story told by the Reverse Mortgage Professional)

For quite some time, I have been helping my senior client, Julie, through her tough financial situation. As a 66 year old lady, she lives by herself and has tried hard to make ends meet on a small monthly income from Social Security. But despite her best efforts, she was falling short by a few hundred dollars each month. It seemed like such a small amount of money, but a few hundred dollars each month starts to add up over the years. To make matters worse, Julie suffers from major back problems and has endured multiple operations to help alleviate the pain. Like so many other seniors, her medical bills were the source of her financial troubles.

It was terrible that there was just not enough money for Julie to make ends meet. Everyone who knew Julie felt sorry for her. Fighting an uphill battle on an almost daily basis starts to take its toll on a person, and it affected Julie's entire life, including her self esteem. She'd often make comments like, "Oh! You know. I'm just not a good person because I can't support myself and need help." It was a shame to see Julie's glowing personality shadowed by deteriorating self confidence and negative feelings about herself.

People from our church and I did our best to build up Julie's opinion of herself all while trying not to make it look like we felt sorry for her, which at times was not easy. Honestly, we did feel sorry for her and the situation she was in. How could you not? But I want everyone reading this story to know we offered help to Julie because we cared for her not because we felt sorry for her.

For years, we did everything we could to help her. We helped by paying a few bills here and there and delivering food to her, especially during the holiday season. It was important for us to help so Julie could try to pay her mortgage each month. She wanted to stay in her house as long as her health allowed her to, and quite honestly, she didn't have the money to move anyway.

After being in the title insurance business for many years, I took a giant leap of faith and entered the reverse mortgage business. Once I'd been in the reverse mortgage business for about a year, I spoke to Julie and suggested a reverse mortgage as a solution to her problems.

The first question I always ask a prospective client when discussing a reverse mortgage is, "Would you like to stay in your home for the foreseeable future?" The answer is always, "Yes." Julie's answer was no different. Julie's brother played a significant role in her decision-making process, and he was extremely concerned about her financial situation. Once he learned about reverse mortgages and how one could benefit his sister, he told Julie this solution was an answer to both of their prayers.

When Julie and I met to gather information for her reverse mortgage application, she was happy. I could see excitement in her eyes and consequently, she could not wait to begin the process. With her brother's blessing, Julie completed the application and scheduled the required HUD counseling, but that was the easy part. Due to years of money being too tight and her back problems, her house was in need of significant repairs. However, even though her home needed repairs, I still suspected Julie had built up enough equity that could be used to supplement her income to make up the shortfall each month.

We moved forward with the appraisal process to get a better idea of what repairs were needed. The house needed a new heater and a roof which cost approximately $15,000. Thankfully, Julie's home appraised for $145,000 which would allow her to pay for the new heater and roof and have money left over each month to supplement her income – and would eliminate her mortgage payment forever.

I called a few contractors, reviewed their bids, and negotiated payment terms with both contractors. They were aware of Julie's specific circumstances and understood their work had to be completed first before Julie's reverse mortgage could be finalized and they could be paid. Both contractors agreed to work with us so we could keep Julie in her home.

This experience had a positive impact on so many aspects of Julie's life. She doesn't have to worry about her finances anymore nor does she have to worry about her roof leaking or her heater not working. She has enough money for her expenses, and she can stay in her house for the remainder of her life. Julie's reverse mortgage has also done wonders to boost her self esteem. She is now so full of pride that she was able to obtain a reverse mortgage (and find a solution to her financial troubles) and all because she owned her house.

This has just been an absolute blessing for Julie, and helping people through situations like these is what makes my job so much fun! This is not your dress rehearsal!

About Joe Kiefer

Barclay Funding Corp.
856-547-2005
joe@njreverse.com

Joe Kiefer was in the real estate and title insurance business for 39 years before falling in love with the reverse mortgage business. As a senior, Joe understands the fears and needs of seniors especially in this troubled economy. Joe's office does reverse mortgages only – nothing else!

Chapter

60

Anthony Lo Schiavo
Apex Lending Incorporated

SAVING BARBARA'S HOME

(Story told by the Reverse Mortgage Professional)

Quite a bit of my marketing efforts involve education. Most people do not understand the concept of a reverse mortgage, and unfortunately, they believe many common myths. I conducted a reverse mortgage presentation for a group of referral sources. Each of the participants thought the reverse mortgage products described were phenomenal tools. They commented about how they had heard about them, but no one had ever explained it the way that I did.

The next week, one gentleman who attended my presentation met with a long-time family friend who told him that his mother was losing her home due to foreclosure. Over the past few months, his 73 year old mother had been packing up her home and was preparing to move out. She had no hope of saving her home as she did not have any money. He continued to share that he had been looking at places for his mom to rent, but she could not even afford to pay for rent unless she went without groceries and medicine.

This is how I met Barbara, my senior client. I was contacted to see if a reverse mortgage could save Barbara's home and to see if I'd be willing to help her through this incredibly stressful time. I immediately scheduled a phone appointment to speak with both the son and the mother, during which they shared the rest of their emotional story with me.

Barbara's son and daughter-in-law told me her home was in foreclosure which was why she was putting all of her belongings in boxes. Over the years, money kept getting tighter and tighter and just never seemed like enough to make ends meet. She thought Social Security would be enough to live on in her golden years, but she quickly learned it was not. The thought of losing her family's home was unbearable. Barbara had lived in this home for over 40 years. She and her husband raised their children in this home, and her husband died in this home. It was clear to me that Barbara was a nervous wreck. She was losing her house to foreclosure, she did not want to move out of her house, and she didn't know what to do.

Living on such a limited budget, to move out and give up her two dogs and three birds along with most of her personal belongings to fit into a small apartment would be a huge task that was overwhelming to think about. Barbara and her son decided that they would research Section 8 housing. It made her son sick to think of his mother living in government housing, especially after viewing a few rental properties. How could Barbara go from living in her family home to living in a run-down efficiency apartment? What kind of life is that for someone who is 73 years old?

We went over what a reverse mortgage was and all the ins and outs of it. At times, Barbara's son would ask, "Is this really true? Are you pulling our string here?" But by the end of our conversation, they fully understood and could not believe that a program like this existed. They had heard about it, but they did not pursue it as an option. Like many others, Barbara perceived a reverse mortgage to be nothing more than a scam and thought that the bank was going to take the house. I outlined next steps, and with renewed hope, Barbara and her son got busy scheduling the required HUD counseling while I made arrangements for the property to be appraised.

The appraisal came back with good news. There would be enough money to pay off Barbara's entire mortgage and keep her home. We did have to jump through one hoop. There was a hole going through the floor of the home through which grass was actually growing. We needed to get the flooring repaired.

We got a contractor's bid, and Barbara's son paid for the work upfront since his mom didn't' have the money. Once the work was done, we were able to release the money to our client. But when Barbara had her money her son did not want his money back.

We were able to save Barbara's home from foreclosure, and once she achieved a reverse mortgage, her son said, "Thank you so much. You've really changed our lives."

Barbara did not unpack anything until we actually closed because she still didn't quite believe that there was a program this good. When we finally closed, she said the first thing she did was to unpack all of the family pictures and put them back on the wall.

Now that Barbara doesn't have a mortgage payment, she can use her Social Security for groceries, medicine, and basic living expenses. A reverse mortgage really did save Barbara's home, and in my opinion, I feel we also prolonged her life. We gave her peace once more because she no longer had to fret over finances. She and her son didn't have to worry about how to make ends meet or about moving her into government housing that would have been an eighteen month wait just to get.

Working with Barbara and her son was really a life-changing event for me. In fact, it was one of the first reverse mortgages that I ever originated. The power of being able to help a 73-year-old woman keep her home and give her peace of mind was an amazing experience for me. To this day it continues to fuel my passion for offering reverse mortgage products and helping seniors.

About Anthony LoSchiavo

Apex Lending Incorporated
866-393-5752
www.aloschiavo.apexlending.com

Anthony Loschiavo has been a top producer with Apex Lending Incorporated since February of 1999. As an independent owner of a commercial location, Anthony and his team originate commercial mortgages, reverse mortgages, home equity loans, and first mortgages.

Chapter
61

Milo Schauer
Umax Mortgage

MAKING ENDS MEET AGAIN

(Story told by the Reverse Mortgage Professional)

Born in Charlestown, South Carolina, Elizabeth is a southern lady through-and-through. What struck me about her when we first met was how attractive, vibrant, and alive she was. Elizabeth is a genuine person who does not hide her feelings.

Elizabeth and her husband, Gailen, were married for 28 years. He started his career in 1945 by serving in the United States Army and then went to work for a large, well-known bank until he retired. Gailen experienced major health issues later in their marriage and subsequently had numerous operations. The last one - an open heart surgery - claimed his life.

Despite Gailen's medical issues, they had an active and good life up until a few weeks before his final surgery. They were smart about their finances, and Gailen even had a $500,000 insurance policy on his life specifically for Elizabeth's benefit should he pass away due to his medical issues.

Those weeks before Gailen's open heart surgery were tough, and Elizabeth could tell he was starting to battle dementia. This was confirmed after he passed away when she discovered that Gailen had cancelled his life insurance policy days before his open heart surgery. Apparently, he no longer wanted to pay the monthly premium and did not think through how the decision would impact his wife's future. He was very ill and because of that, could not be held responsible for his actions.

Now in her 70s, Elizabeth was faced with the death of her husband, how to pay for Gailen's funeral expenses, and how to make ends meet for the rest of her life. After Gailen's estate was settled, Elizabeth was left with the property and a small Social Security pension benefit. Even though Gailen worked for the same large bank for years, as the spouse of the deceased, Elizabeth's Social Security was limited.

Elizabeth was left with less than $1,000 a month to live on. She was very concerned about her future and needed to figure out her options. That's what prompted her to start thinking about a reverse mortgage.

Elizabeth saw a television commercial hosted by a national company using a famous celebrity to advertise reverse mortgages. She just did not feel comfortable working with a company located across the country.

Meanwhile, I did a routine mailing to a group of senior clients in my general market area, and one of the recipients was a friend of Elizabeth's. My letter was written with the specific intention of creating an open dialogue with my reader, emphasizing my integrity, trust, and experience. I think that came through because my letter was passed to Elizabeth.

When Elizabeth called me, she explained her circumstances and gave me all the information that I needed to put together a proper quotation for her. From there, we made arrangements to meet. She asked if it would be possible for her daughter to attend the meeting. I told her that not only was it possible, but I encouraged her to invite her daughter to attend.

We met at Elizabeth's house and went over all of the documents. I outlined all the provisions of her reverse mortgage and she was very much in favor of it. Conversely, Elizabeth's daughter was concerned about her mother entering into a reverse mortgage. She did not fully understand how it worked and thought it meant that her mother would lose the house. However, once I was able to clarify the truth for her, it was no longer an issue. She realized that her mother needed the additional income and was supportive of the decision.

Elizabeth was adamant that she needed at least an additional $500 a month to help her pay bills, but she also wanted to make sure that she was able to leave both of her daughters with an inheritance. As if Gailen was helping from above, when I worked the numbers out, it came out to exactly what Elizabeth needed. I was able to provide her with $500 a month from her reverse mortgage. Additionally, she would be able to leave both of her daughters a sizeable inheritance.

Those numbers made Elizabeth comfortable. She was going to be able to accomplish all of her financial objectives. She also wanted to make sure that her daughters were both protected, so a revocable living trust was set up prior to closing the escrow, where both of her daughters are beneficiaries under the trust.

Elizabeth believes strongly in her decision of achieving a reverse mortgage as well as working with me. She has referred me to many of her friends and has even arranged for me to make a presentation to the ladies of her church. It is important to me that my clients have that kind of confidence. As a fellow senior, I truly understand their needs, and I strive to make sure each client can trust me implicitly.

Just like with all of my clients, I have made it a point to tell Elizabeth she is welcome to call me at any time with questions. If I have the answer, I will give her the answer. And if I do not, I will find the answer. In other words, I will become an advocate for anything she needs, not just the reverse mortgage, making Elizabeth my client for life.

About Milo Schauer

Umax Mortgage
541-580-7747
eureka05@charter.net
www.umaxmortgage.com/mschauer

As a Reverse Mortgage Specialist working in the Senior Products market, my background and life experiences have provided me with the necessary skills to understand the needs, wants, and desires of our senior clients. Being a senior myself, I am dedicated to our company's concept of: "Experience, Trust, and Integrity".

We are all facing difficult and challenging times in our financial lives. As a seasoned financial advisor, I pledge to be your advocate in helping you obtaining the best loan product available.

Chapter

62

Phillis Jackson
Athan Mortgage

A GIFT OF LIFESTYLE OPPORTUNITY

(Story told by the Reverse Mortgage Professional)

Twenty years ago, John and Helen owned a small business that did not survive. They lost the business and in the process, ended up owing quite a bit of business related taxes to the state of Texas. Over the years, John and Helen paid what they could, but ultimately they could never quite get their debt under control which resulted in the state putting a lien against their property.

To put it mildly, they were worried. John was probably more depressed about the situation than Helen simply because he felt that the man's role was to be able to take care of his family. However, taking care of his family was becoming more difficult as they were both in their late 70s. Age (who was going to hire someone in their 70s?) coupled with a mortgage payment that had grown to over $1,700 per month. This because the adjustable rate mortgage they had on their original mortgage that started at 3.3% had grown to 8.8% and was close to becoming unmanageable. In addition to the outstanding tax bills, it all just seemed like too much to bear.

Unsure of where to turn, John and Helen made an appointment to meet with a bankruptcy attorney. After reviewing their situation, the bankruptcy attorney wanted to see if there was an alternative to Helen and John filing for bankruptcy. The attorney called me as he was curious if a reverse mortgage would be a good solution for John and Helen.

As it turns out, John and Helen owned a very nice property. In fact, their home was appraised at over $350,000. John came to my office first by himself. Together, we reviewed his situation and discussed how a reverse mortgage might benefit him and his wife in this trying time. John immediately felt a reverse mortgage would be the way to go, but when he took the information home and talked to Helen about it, she was completely against it.

Helen thought that it (a reverse mortgage) was one of those things that was "too good to be true," and John was too worried about their situation to make a good decision. Helen made it clear that she was opposed to pursuing a reverse mortgage.

Conversely, John felt a reverse mortgage would be the only way to free up $1,700 per month in cash and use that money to pay back their past due taxes. They could ultimately get the lien removed from their property. John decided to have me begin the process knowing that Helen would eventually get on board with this solution.

Our first hurdle was to get the title company to take the past due state taxes off the title. It is important to note that the past due taxes would not be forgiven; they would just be put on hold (and the lien removed from the title temporarily) until the reverse mortgage was final. To complicate matters even more, the past due taxes were extremely old and because within the state of Texas, their primary residence was a homestead, in theory the state could just make John and Helen pay the past due taxes out of the funds that they were going to get from their reverse mortgage. In addition, the State of Texas compounded the problem by adding a 10% penalty every year on the judgment. Unfortunately or *maybe fortunately*, John and Helen were not going to receive any funds at closing. They were in fact, going to have to bring funds to closing to help in the paying off their current mortgage.

For the next three or four months, I worked with the State, the attorney and the title company trying to get the above concessions implemented. Thankfully, we were finally able to get them to agree to our requests. This was a huge opportunity for John and Helen and because of this, Helen finally decided that a reverse mortgage could be a good solution for them. Helen explained her hesitation stemmed from not believing it was even possible, especially on account of the hurdles with the state. Now that she could see a way out of their financial hardship, Helen was on board with the entire plan.

John and Helen's reverse mortgage has completely changed their lives. While they still owe those past due taxes, they are working on paying them back. John was so impressed with the concept of a reverse mortgage and my approach to working with seniors he now works for me as a loan officer!

John's business knowledge coupled with his personal experience has made him a true advocate for seniors utilizing a reverse mortgage to better their lives. John explains a reverse mortgage in terms that make seniors comfortable and understands the concept of this complicated mortgage product. People like to talk to him not only because he is now 80 years old and leads quite an active lifestyle, but his experience in obtaining his reverse mortgage gives him a firm foundation of understanding of reverse mortgages. He truly is a testament of how beneficial a reverse mortgage truly can be.

John recently launched a television campaign in which John is the star. You should see John on television, telling people about his story and inviting them to call him to see if a reverse mortgage could help them achieve financial independence.

A reverse mortgage changed John and Helen's life forever. John now has a new career, has reduced his debt, and is loving life.

About Phillis Jackson

www.AmarilloReverseMortgage.com
806-352-9260

As Manager of Athlan Mortgage, a branch of Network Funding LP, Phillis Jackson closed the **first** Reverse Mortgage in Amarillo, TX (the second one in Texas) and **has a heart for working with Seniors.** She has over 26 years experience in the field of Real Estate, specializing in investing and financing real property for over 18 years. Phillis teaches "Financial Update" at Amarillo College for the Texas Real Estate licensee's MCE requirements. Ms. Jackson is a regular guest on KGNC Radio, 710 on the dial, "The Financial Clinic" Saturday mornings 10:00 to 12:00 AM where she interacts with the public through questions about reverse mortgages.

Reverse Mortgage Basics

Reverse mortgages are helping older Americans across the country achieve greater financial security and enjoy their retirement years to the fullest.

For those new to the concept, reverse mortgages are loans that can be used by senior homeowners ages 62 and older to convert the equity in their home into a usable cash asset. The reverse mortgage is funded by a lending institution such as a mortgage lender, bank, credit union, or savings and loan association.

The only reverse mortgage insured by the U.S. Federal Government is called a Home Equity Conversion Mortgage (HECM). Specifically, the Federal Housing Administration—commonly known as the FHA—is the insuring agent. One key benefit to a HECM is that it requires homeowners to receive consumer education and counseling by a HUD-approved HECM counselor to help homeowners decide if this type of program would meet their needs.

During these educational sessions, HECM counselors discuss program eligibility requirements, financial implications and alternatives to obtaining an HECM, and provisions for the mortgage becoming due and payable. Upon the completion of HECM counseling, the home-owner should be able to make an independent, informed decision of whether this product will meet their needs. You can also use HUD's handy Reverse Mortgage Calculator to help you see if you qualify.

Homeowners who meet the eligibility criteria can complete a reverse mortgage application by contacting an FHA-approved lending institution. If you need assistance locating an FHA-approved lender, you can request a listing of approved lenders from the HECM counselor or use HUD's searchable listing.

Borrower Requirements:

- ☐ Aged 62 years or older
- ☐ Own your property
- ☐ Occupy your property as primary residence
- ☐ Participate in a consumer information session given by an approved HECM counselor
- ☐ Mortgage Amount Based On:
    - * Age of the youngest borrower
    - * Current interest rate
    - * Lesser of appraised value or the FHA insurance limit

Financial Requirements:

- ☐ No income or credit qualifications are required of the borrower
- ☐ No repayment as long as the property is the primary residence
- ☐ Most closing costs may be financed in the mortgage

Property Requirements:

- ☐ Single-family home or two- to four-unit homes with one unit occupied by the borrower

☐   HUD-approved condominiums

☐   Manufactured homes and leased land

☐   Meet FHA property standards and flood requirements

How the Home Equity Conversion Mortgage (HECM) Program Works:

Homeowners 62 years of age and older who have paid off their mortgages or have only small mortgage balances remaining, and who currently use the property as a primary residence are eligible to participate in HUD's reverse mortgage program.

The program allows homeowners to borrow against the equity in their homes. Homeowners can select from five payment plans:

1. Tenure—equal monthly payments as long as at least one borrower lives and continues to occupy the property as a principal residence.

2. Term—equal monthly payments for a fixed number of months selected.

3. Line of Credit—unscheduled payments or in installments, at times and in amount of borrower's choosing until the line of credit is exhausted.

4. Modified Tenure—line of credit combined with monthly payments for as long as the borrower remains in the home.

5. Modified Term—line of credit combined with monthly payments for a fixed number of months selected by the borrower.

Homeowners whose circumstances change can restructure their payment options for a nominal fee, which may vary depending on the lender.

Unlike ordinary home equity loans, a HUD HECM reverse mortgage does not require repayment as long as the home is the borrower's principal residence. Lenders recover their principal, plus interest, when the home is sold. The remaining value of the home goes to the homeowner or to his or her survivors. You can never owe more than your home's value.

If the sales proceeds are insufficient to pay the amount owed, HUD will pay the lender the amount of the shortfall. The FHA collects an insurance premium from all borrowers to provide this coverage. This is the beauty of the HUD's FHA guarantee.

The amount a homeowner can borrow depends on their age, the current interest rate, other loan fees and the appraised value of their home or FHA's mortgage limits for their area, whichever is less. Generally, the more valuable your home is and the older you are the more you can borrow.

There are no asset or income limitations on borrowers receiving HUD's HECM reverse mortgages. This means to qualify, homeowners are not required to hold a certain amount of assets, and income is not a factor.

There are also no limits on the value of homes qualifying for a HUD HECM reverse mortgage. The value of the home will be determined by an appraisal. However, the amount that may be borrowed is derived from the lower of the appraisal amount or FHA mortgage limit.

HUD collects funds from insurance premiums charged homeowners who receive HECM mortgages. Homeowners are charged an upfront insurance premium, which is 2 percent of the maximum claim amount that may be borrowed plus a .5 percent annual premium.

More Questions:

If you have questions, a member of the Seniors Right to Know Network will be glad to assist you. Visit www.seniorsrighttoknow.org and click on your state and the city nearest to you. You may also email us at info@seniorsrighttoknow.org or call us at 1-800-242-5085.

Top 10 Questions About Reverse Mortgages

Since your home is probably your largest single investment, it's smart to know more about reverse mortgages before deciding if one is right for you! Your Seniors Right to Know Network reverse mortgage professionals are ready to provide you with more answers.

1. What is a reverse mortgage?

A reverse mortgage is a special type of home loan that lets a homeowner convert a portion of the equity in his or her home into cash. Your home's equity, built up over years of making home mortgage payments, can be paid to you. But unlike a traditional home equity loan or second mortgage, no repayment is required until the borrower(s) no longer use the home as their principal residence. HUD's reverse mortgage provides these benefits, and it is federally insured as well.

2. Can I qualify for a HUD reverse mortgage?

To be eligible for a HUD-endorsed reverse mortgage, the FHA requires the borrower: be a homeowner, 62 years of age or older; own your home outright, or have a low mortgage balance that can be paid off at the closing with proceeds from the reverse loan; and live in the home. You are further required to receive consumer information from HUD-approved counseling sources prior to obtaining the loan. A reverse mortgage professional can also visit you to help you with these resources.

3. Can I apply if I didn't buy my present house with FHA mortgage insurance?

Yes. It doesn't matter if you didn't buy it with an FHA-insured mortgage. Your new HUD reverse mortgage will be a new FHA-insured mortgage loan.

4. What types of homes are eligible?

Your home must be a single-family dwelling or a two- to four-unit property that you own and occupy. Townhouses, detached homes, units in condominiums and some manufactured homes, and some co-ops are also eligible. Condominiums must be FHA-approved. It is possible for individual condominium units to qualify under the Spot Loan program. Individual lenders give specific guidelines.

5. What's the difference between a reverse mortgage and a bank home equity loan?

With a traditional second mortgage or a home equity line of credit, you must have sufficient income versus debt ratio to qualify for the loan, and you are required to make monthly mortgage payments.

The reverse mortgage is different in that your line of credit does not require a monthly payment, and the unused portion can actually grow and is available regardless of your current income. The amount you can borrow depends on your age, the current interest rate, and the appraised value of your home or FHA's mortgage limits for your area, whichever is less.

Generally, the value of your home, your current age, and the current interest rate will determine how much you can borrow. You don't make payments, because the loan is not due as long as the house is your principal residence. Like all homeowners, you still are required to pay your real estate taxes and other conventional payments like utilities, but with an FHA-insured HUD reverse mortgage, you cannot be foreclosed or forced to vacate your house because you "missed your mortgage payment." Obviously, you must still do routine maintenance and keep your home in good order.

6. Can the lender take my home away if I outlive the loan?

No! You do not need to repay the loan as long as you or one of the borrowers continues to live in the house and keeps the taxes, insurance current, and maintenance. You can never owe more than your home's value.

7. Will I still have an estate that I can leave to my heirs?

When you sell your home or no longer use it for your primary residence, you or your estate will repay the cash you received from the reverse mortgage, plus interest and other fees, to the lender. The remaining equity in your home, if any, belongs to you or to your heirs. This feature is called non-recourse and is the protection you purchase with FHA mortgage insurance.

8. How much money can I get from my home?

The amount you can borrow depends on your age, the current interest rate, and the appraised value of your home or FHA's mortgage limits for your area, whichever is less. Generally, the more valuable your home is and the older you are, the more you can borrow.

9. I've been contacted by a firm that will give me the name of a lender for a "small percentage" of the loan. Should I use that firm or an estate planning service to find a reverse mortgage?

We do NOT recommend using an estate planning service or any service that charges a fee just for referring a borrower to a lender!

10. How do I receive my payments?

You have five options:

1. Tenure—equal monthly payments as long as at least one borrower lives and continues to occupy the property as a principal residence.
2. Term—equal monthly payments for a fixed number of months selected.
3. Line of Credit—unscheduled payments or in installments, at times and in amounts of borrower's choosing until the line of credit is exhausted.
4. Modified Tenure—line of credit combined with monthly payments for as long as the borrower remains in the home.

5. Modified Term—line of credit combined with monthly payments for a fixed number of months selected by the borrower.

You probably have other questions and concerns. We understand. To assist you with any other questions, please contact your local Seniors Right to Know Network representative by visiting www.seniorsrightoknow.org.

Purchase a Home Using a Reverse Mortgage

If you've made the decision to purchase your principal residence using loan proceeds from a reverse mortgage, you may still have questions. Below are those most frequently asked.

Contacting your local Seniors Right to Know Network reverse mortgage professional is also a good place to start when considering a purchase using a reverse mortgage. Visit www.SeniorsRightToKnow.org for more information.

1. What is an HECM (reverse mortgage) for Purchase?

HECM for Purchase allows seniors, ages 62 or older, to purchase a new principal residence using loan proceeds from the reverse mortgage.

2. What is the purpose of the program?

The program was designed to allow seniors to purchase a new principal residence and obtain a reverse mortgage within a single transaction by eliminating the need for a second closing. The program was also designed to enable senior homeowners to relocate to other geographical areas to be closer to family members or downsize to homes that meet their physical needs, i.e., handrails, one-level properties, ramps, wider doorways, and so forth.

3. Can clients who are interested in an HECM for Purchase transaction receive HUD-approved housing counseling agency?

Yes. Counseling on HECM for Purchase transactions is available effective January 1, 2009.

4. What property types are ineligible?

- Cooperative units
- Newly constructed residences where a Certificate of Occupancy or its equivalent has not been issued by the appropriate local authority
- Boarding houses
- Bed and breakfast establishments
- Existing manufactured homes built before June 15, 1976
- Existing manufactured homes built after June 15, 1976, which fail to conform to the Manufactured Home Construction Safety Standards, as evidenced by affixed certification labels (e.g., data plate and HUD certification label) and/or lack a permanent foundation as required in HUD's Permanent Foundations for Manufactured Housing Guide

For additional information about HECM purchases, please contact your local Seniors Right to Know Network representative: www.SeniorsRightToKnow.org

Click on your state for the nearest Seniors Right to Know Network professional nearest you.

We can be reached via email at info@seniorsrighttoknow.org or telephone at 1-800-242-5085.

Important Resources for Seniors Interested in HECM (Reverse Mortgage)

HUD Counseling

Increasing demand for HECM reverse mortgages by senior citizens has put pressure on the counseling industry to meet the demand for the required counseling. To make sufficient quality Home Equity Conversion Mortgage (HECM) counseling available, HECM counselors from the below agencies are permitted to provide face-to-face and telephone counseling nationally. Please contact them to obtain HECM counseling.

National Foundation for Credit Counseling (NFCC), 1-866-698-6322

Money Management International (MMI), 1-877-908-2227

American Association of Retired Persons (AARP), 1-800-209-8085

To find local HUD information by city and state, go to this link: http://www.hud.gov/local/index.cfm

Additional Questions?

If you have additional questions, a member of the Seniors Right to Know Network will be glad to assist you. Click on your state and the city nearest you. Feel free to email us at info@seniorsrighttoknow.org or call us at 1-800-242-5085.

Reverse Mortgage Terms

adjustable rate - an interest rate that changes, based on changes in a published market-rate index

application - this is when you meet with your reverse mortgage professional to start the reverse mortgage process, review disclosures, programs, examples, and begin the HECM reverse mortgage process

appraisal - an estimate of much a house would sell for if it were sold; also called its market value. HECM appraisals are completed by FHA approved appraisers

appreciation - an increase in a home's value

cap - a limit on the amount an adjustable interest rate may go up or down during a specified time period

closing - a meeting where documents are signed to "close the deal" on a mortgage; the time a mortgage begins

CMT – Constant Maturity Treasury

counseling - to be eligible for a HECM, Reverse Mortgage, federally insured, you must discuss the loan with a counselor employed by a nonprofit or public agency approved by the U.S. Department of Housing and Urban Development, (HUD) A requirement for all HECM borrowers

credit line - a credit account that lets a borrower decide when to take money out and also how much to take out; also known as a "line-of-credit" or "credit line."

current interest rate - in the HECM program, the interest rate currently being charged on a loan.

depreciation - a decrease in the value of a home

expected interest rate - in the HECM program, the interest rate used to determine a borrower's loan advance amounts; it equals the 10-year rate for U.S. Treasury Securities, plus a margin.

Fannie Mae - a private company that buys and sells mortgages; a government-sponsored business that is watched over by the federal government

Federal Housing Administration (FHA) - the part of the U. S. Department of Housing and Urban Development (HUD) that insures HECM loans

federally insured reverse mortgage - a reverse mortgage guaranteed by the federal government so you will always get what the loan promises

fixed monthly loan advances - payments of the same amount that is made to a borrower each month

forward mortgage - this reference is used for traditional loans, such as a regular purchase, regular refinance, traditional line of credit, or home equity loans; all of which require a monthly payment, proof of income and credit requirements.

home equity - the value of a home, subtracting any money owed on it

Home Equity Conversion Mortgage (HECM) - the only reverse mortgage program insured by the Federal Housing Administration, a federal government agency

initial interest rate - in the HECM program, the interest rate that is first charged on the loan beginning at closing; it equals the one-year rate for U.S. Treasury Securities, plus a margin

LIBOR - The London Interbank Offered Rate (or LIBOR) is a daily reference rate based on the interest rates at which banks offer to lend unsecured funds

loan balance - the amount owed, including principal and interest

lump sum - a single loan advance at the time of a loan closing

margin - in the HECM program, the amount added to the one-year Treasury rate to determine the initial and current interest rates, and to the 10-year Treasury rate to determine the expected interest rate

mortgage - a legal document making a home available as security for a lender to repay a debt

non-recourse mortgage - a home loan in which the borrower can never owe more than the home's value at the time the loan is repaid

origination - the process of setting up a mortgage, including preparing documents

proprietary reverse mortgage - a reverse mortgage product owned and offered by a private company

reverse mortgage - common term for FHA HECM – Home Equity Conversion Mortgage

right of rescission - a borrower's right to cancel a home loan within three business days of the loan closing

servicing - administering a loan after closing, such as maintaining loan records and sending statements

tenure advances - fixed monthly loan advances for as long as a borrower lives in their primary home

term advances - fixed monthly loan advances for a specific period of time advanced to a borrower who lives in their primary home

Total Annual Loan Cost (TALC) rate - the projected total annual average cost of a reverse mortgage including all itemized costs

T-rate - the rate for U.S. Treasury Securities; used to determine the initial, expected, and current interest rates for the HECM program

MORE QUESTIONS:

Clarification & explanations for any of these terms will be reviewed when you meet or call your Reverse Mortgage Professional.

For your FREE Report or DVD video, call your local Senior Right to Know Member, at 800-242-5085 or visit www.SeniorsRightToKnow.org or www.62SeniorMoments.com

RESOURCES

American Society on Aging

http://www.asaging.org

A network of professionals in the field of aging that provides education and information on the latest developments.

Benefits Checkup

http://www.benefitscheckup.org

Helps seniors identify public programs for which they may be eligible. This group also connects seniors to federal and state programs.

Eldercare Locator

http://www.eldercare.gov

Assists seniors in finding services and programs in their area.

First Gov for Seniors

http://www.seniors.gov

Provides online access to government information and services of interest to seniors.

Seniors Right To Know Network

http://www.seniorsrighttoknow.org

This site provides free, accessible online information about reverse mortgages. The website lists participating members of the Seniors Right to Know Network for seniors to locate a reverse mortgage professional in their state. Seniors may also receive a free report and free DVD.

62 Senior Moments

http://www.62SeniorMoments.com

Re-order 62 Senior Moments for a friend, contact a contributing author, or email a question.

National Reverse Mortgage Lenders Associations

http://www.nrmla.org

This advocacy group serves as the voice for lenders and investors and helps educate consumers about reverse mortgages.

Senior Discounts

http://www.seniordiscounts.com

The most complete and accurate listing of all senior-related discounts for goods and services throughout the United States.

Homeless

http://www.hud.gov/homeless/index.cfm

This website provides assistances for the homeless or for those who wish to help the homeless.

The National Council on Aging

http://www.ncoa.org

This nonprofit agency helps improve the health of seniors through education and awareness programs implemented in conjunction with communities, churches, consumer groups, business, labor and local government agencies.

USA Gov

http://www.usa.gov/Topics/Seniors.shtml

Various resources are available on this website to assist seniors.

Housing Assistance

http://www.hud.gov/groups/seniors.cfm

Provides resources and guides to help seniors make the right decision about their living arrangements in their golden years.

Reverse Mortgages Information from HUD

http://www.hud.gov/buying/rvrsmort.cfm

Extensive and detailed information about reverse mortgages.

Free report from HUD

http://www.hud.gov/offices/hsg/sfh/hecm/rmtopten.cfm

A free report from HUD to help seniors in their decision making.

AARP

http://www.aarp.org

This website is filled with information for seniors.

Administration on Housing

http://www.aoa.gov/eldfam/Housing/Housing.aspx

Additional information about housing options for seniors.

Alliance for Retired Americans

http://www.retiredamericans.org/

Provides valuable information to seniors on policies, politics and institutions that affect their lives.

Social Security

http://www.ssa.gov/

Online tools for benefits and information from the Social Security Administration.

GET YOUR FREE DVD

☐ Please send my FREE DVD
"All About Reverse Mortgages"

Homeowners First Name(s) _____

Homeowners Last Name (s) _____

Address _____

City   _____

State   _____

Zip   _____

Phone   _____

Email   _____

Date of Birth _____

(both homeowners)

Mortgage Balance (if any) _____

Current Home Value _____

TO GET YOUR DVD,
SIMPLY CHOSE ONE THE OPTIONS BELOW:

PHONE: (800) 242-5085
FAX DVD request to (302) 266-7660
EMAIL to info@seniorsrighttoknow.org

62 SENIOR MOMENTS BOOK

$19.95 per book plus $5.95 shipping = $25.90

I would like to order _____ books.

Total Order $ _____

* *

Name _____

Address _____

City, State, Zip _____

Phone _____

Email _____

Card Number _____

Visa _____ MC _____ AMEX _____ Discover _____

Exp. Date: _____ 3 or 4 security _____

Signature: _____

PLEASE MAIL THIS ORDER FORM TO:

62 Senior Moments Book
22 Polly Drummond Hill Road
Newark, DE 19711

FAX your order to: (302)266-7660
PHONE in your order by calling (800)242-5085
ORDER ONLINE on our secure server www.62seniormoments.com